Is it Kosher?

IS IT KOSHER?

ENCYCLOPEDIA OF
KOSHER FOODS FACTS & FALLACIES

By Rabbi E. Eidlitz

FELDHEIM PUBLISHERS Jerusalem / New York

First published 1992
Hardcover edition: ISBN 0-87306-606-5
Second Edition — 1993
Third Edition — 1995
Copyright © 1992 by
Rabbi E. Eidlitz and Feldheim Publishers Ltd.

Phototypeset by Susan Dolin Graphics

Feldheim Publishers
POB 35002 / Jerusalem, Israel

200 Airport Executive Park
Nanuet, NY 10954

Printed in Israel

Dedicated to my wife Devorah
and our children
Adina and Viggi, Reuven,
Yehoshua, Yehudis, Rivki, and Atara Ita

TABLE OF CONTENTS

TABLE OF CONTENTS

PREFACE

This book was written primarily with the kosher consumer in mind. Whether a person is thoroughly well-versed in the laws of kashrus or a frustrated novice, the applicability of these laws today is exceedingly confusing. Prior to the food revolution of over 50 years ago, most food was grown or processed by the person or family who would be eating it. If a person wanted a variety of dairy products, they simply would go to their barn, milk the cow and have the raw material to make butter or cheese. All, of course, would be natural, without added ingredients. What you saw is what you got. Today, this has changed greatly with technology. It is perfectly feasible for a strictly kosher consumer to eat a "cheeseburger with milkshake" without doing anything wrong. The milk could be from soybeans (pareve) the cheese could be from soybeans (pareve), the ice cream could be from soybeans (pareve), the ice cream for the milkshake could be from soybeans (pareve); and as a matter of fact, even the bread could be made from soybean. On the other hand, a simple item such as grade B butter could be made from non-kosher sour cream, contain various coloring, or it may just look like butter but actually be margarine, which could contain many non-kosher ingredients.

Indeed, during these past few years, food technology has led to a kosher food industry which expanded from a backyard operation to an industry approaching $30 billion in sales annually.

It is our hope and prayer that this book will serve as a practical source of information to anyone interested in kosher foods. It is with much gratitude to Hashem Yisborach that we are publishing this book. Fourteen years of research which combined food technology and halacha have gone into this work. Bearing in mind that many people have different criteria for what they deem acceptable in Kashrus, we have endeavored to explain fully each topic in detail and to remove some of the mystery associated with kashrus. Although every topic was researched and checked diligently, methods of food technology are prone to change. As with all matters of halacha, when in doubt, check with your local competent rabbi.

Eliezer Eidlitz

ACKNOWLEDGMENTS

I would like to express my deepest gratitude and admiration for my wife, Devorah, for her constant encouragement and help in writing this book. She is a great example of all that chazal depict as a true Aishes Chayil.

I would also like to acknowledge the following people: Harav Yaacov Yitzhock Ruderman, ZT"L who encouraged me to continue this work. Harav Moshe Heineman, Shlita, who has been the source of inspiration and guidance for much of this work.

To Rabbi & Mrs. Dov Aharoni for their expert editing, to Susan Dolin for putting her heart into the typesetting, to Susan Shapiro who helped in the early stages of this book development, and to my wonderful in-laws, Mr. and Mrs. Wolin , who have been as dear as parents to me, tirelessly proofreading the entire manuscript.

To Rabbi Yochanan Stepen, for his guidance, encouragement, and above all, tolerance of my preoccupation with writing this book.

To my dear father, Mr. Yaacov Eidlitz, 'שיח for his many years of help and guidance.

Many thanks to Debbie Remer, for her many hours of dedicated review of the final manuscript.

Last of all, my deepest gratitude to Ron Frisch, who has worked tirelessly and at great expense to ensure the publication of this work.

Rabbi Jacob I. Rudenman

400 Mt. Wilson Lane

Baltimore, MD. 21200

יעקב יצחק הלוי רודרמן

באלטימאר .מד.

ל' תשרי תשמ"ב

באתי להכיר את הרב אליעזר אידליץ הי"ו כי הוא
ת"ח וראוי לסמוך עליו בעניני כשרות כי טרח ועמל
בענינים אלו לברר את כל הנוגע במציאות למעשה
וראוי לתמכו ולסעדו ולחזק את ידיו במה שמפרסם
ומוציא לאור המציאות בעולם הכשרות

הכו"ח

יעקב יצחק הלוי רודרמן

Rabbi Moshe Heinemann
401 Yeshiva Lane
Baltimore, MD 20208
Tel. (801) 484-9079

משה היינעמאן
אב״ד ק״ק אגודת ישראל
באלטימאר
טל. 764-7778 (301)

בס״ד

June 18, 1991

A tremendous amount of research and scholarship has been condensed into this valuable compendium, "IS IT KOSHER?", authored by my colleague, Rabbi Eliezer Eidlitz, shlita.

A wealth of kashrus guidelines, directives and information has been incorporated between its covers.

I am convinced that those who read through the pages of this important work will gain a deeper understanding of the kosher diet and will feel it is a must for the kosher home.

FDA / CFSAN

OFFICE OF FIELD PROGRAMS

200 "C" ST., SW/HFS-600

Room 5001, Washington, DC 20204

Phone #: (202) 205-4187 • FAX #: (202) 205-4819

To Rabbi Eidlitz,

The book, Is it Kosher? Encyclopedia of Kosher Foods Facts and Fallacies is useful in depicting and explaining the various kosher symbols, explaining food additives and other food ingredients and their uses, and in detailing the defect action levels for various foods. I found the section on fish to be of particular interest. This slender volume is truly an encyclopedia with its complete table of contents and detailed index.

Raymond E. Newberry

Deputy Director

U.S. Food and Drug Administration

Division of Regulatory Guidance, HFF-310

INTRODUCTION

T here was a time when a woman did all her family's preparation in her own kitchen. Back then, it was obvious that pig's feet were not kosher, and ice cream was. In the past few decades, however, there has been a revolution in American eating. Almost 90 percent of our food is now processed before reaching our kitchens. With synthetic meats and exotic food additives, artificial pig's feet could be kosher, whereas the ice cream might not be.

These developments in the food industry have been paralleled by the growth of kosher certification organizations formed to assure consumers that appropriately processed foods can be bought with confidence.

As a matter of fact, it has been estimated that approximately one third of all shelf products in our supermarkets are certified kosher. This makes the kosher industry in the U.S. a 30 billion dollars a year business. Although only a relatively small amount of this is dedicated strictly toward the kosher consumer (about $2 billion), the interest in kosher food is rapidly growing. Some adhere to kosher laws from conviction, such as seventh day adventists, Muslims, and vegetarians. However most of the interest comes from people who feel that the kosher certification is their best guarantee that the products and its ingredients are being watched carefully and properly. Some large corporation have found it profitable to acquire kosher companies, such as a recent (1992) acquisition by Sara Lee of the $85 million a year Besin Corp., which produces Sinai and Best products. This trend appears to be on the rise. In the U.S. alone, there appear to be at least 5 million people who buy products based on their being kosher.

A food manufacturer obtains kosher certification usually by requesting it. The reasons for the request can vary from the company's own desire to produce a kosher product to appeals from industrial customers or consumers. Sometimes company "A" requests supervision, and in the course of the investigation of its ingredients it becomes clear that Company "B"s products will also require certification. Some certifying organizations solicit companies. Others, such as the O/U, provide certification only upon application by a food manufacturer.

Once contact with a certifying agency is made, the detective work begins. The manufacturer must supply a complete, detailed list of every ingredient in the product, including preservatives, release agents, stabilizers or other inert ingredients. In addition, every step in the manufacturing process, every cleansing agent used on the equipment and all other products produced on the same premises require close investigating and supervision.

The certifying agency must track down each ingredient to its ultimate source. If, for instance, the ingredient is meat or a meat by-product, the item cannot be kosher unless the meat source itself is strictly kosher. Wine and wine by-products, cheese, and some dairy by-products (such as whey) present the same problem. Any oil used in the manufacture of foodstuffs has to be traced back to the oil processor. Many vegetable oils are produced in machinery that is also used to process animal fats and oils. The Federal Food and Drug Administration acknowledges that "100 percent vegetable oil" may in fact have a percentage of animal fat in some batches. In such a case, of course, the oil is not recommended.

Some ingredients with innocuous sounding names need special attention. "Natural colors" have been known to be derived from insects, "softeners" from whale oil, and "artificial flavors" from cats. Therefore, the supervising agency must conduct a complete and intense investigation into the origin of all the ingredients.

The process by which ingredients are produced must also be carefully checked. In fact, it is necessary to check the processing locations to verify that hygienic standards are not so lax as to allow insects or worms to contaminate the food product. Unfortunately, lax hygiene in food processing is more common than people wish to believe. (See article and listings on page 205.)

The results of all these investigations are forwarded to the rabbinic authority (or board) of the supervising agency. If changes in ingredients or processes are required, the manufacturer must make the changes before the agency will do further work. Once all is acceptable, the rabbinic authority will determine the amount of on-plant supervision necessary. This information is written into a contract and then sent to the manufacturer. The contract also specifies that the manufacturer agrees to make no changes of ingredients or suppliers without prior written consent of the agency. The actual on-site inspector *(mashgiach)* will verify that the company is complying with the contract.

Should the manufacturer cease to comply with the contract, the agency either will see that the necessary changes are made or it will revoke its certification. Because organizations like the O/U or Chaf-K have registered servicemarks, unauthorized printing of these symbols on labels is a violation of Federal law. These certifying agencies have legal redress against possible abuse by manufacturers of their symbols. Some states have laws against falsely advertising that a product is kosher (See chapter on State Regulations.) Also, when reliable certifying agencies know that a particular product will no longer be under their supervision, they will publicize that fact widely. However, these safeguards are not enforceable when only the letter K is used for kosher certification.

The cost of certification to the manufacturer is minimal. For non-profit agencies, cost depends on the amount of on-site work. Agencies making a profit might have a minimum annual charge and fees dependent on the gross annual sales of the product. The individual supervisor *(mashgiach)* is typically paid for each visit he makes to the plant. (He usually receives less per visit than an auto mechanic makes per hour.) The *mashgiach* is paid by the certifying agency and not by the manufacturer. There is usually no increase in the price of the product due to its kosher certification, because the cost of certification is generally met by increased sales. The O/U reports that in over 45 years, fewer than 12 companies discontinued their certification programs because sales did not increase. Thus, kosher supervision benefits the manufacturer and the consumer, who can be confident that foods may be consumed without violating the kosher standards.

If this were the whole story, this chapter would not be necessary. But the fact is that standards, even of national certifying organizations, can vary significantly. Perhaps our suspicion of the legitimacy of the kosher status of some products can be illustrated most clearly with the following actual letter from a certifying rabbi to a food manufacturer. All identifying information has been deleted. The footnotes explain the problems raised by the letter.

January __, ____

_____

_____

_____

Dear Mr. _____,

It was a pleasure to hear from you. I am happy to inform you that I certainly will grant kosher certification to (name of product). You may identify these products with the K insignia.[1] However, I would very much wish[2] to know the names of the suppliers and the ingredients.[3] I expect to be at the _____ plant during February,[4] and perhaps at that time the manufacturing procedure of these new products[5] could be explained to me.[6] With warm and most cordial wishes for all the best, I am.

Sincerely yours,

Rabbi _____

Our notes:

[1] The manufacturer did not need this line to have permission to print a K on the label. The K is not a copyrighted symbol nor even a certification that the product is kosher.

[2] "Wish," not "need"!

[3] The rabbi asks this AFTER stating that the product is kosher. Is he a prophet?

[4] That is, the actual investigation of the product, the manufacturing process, and the ingredients will not be completed for a month. During that time, the manufacturer will—with the rabbi's authorization—be printing K's on his labels, thinking that it is kosher and misleading the public into believing that the product is kosher despite the absence of evidence. Let us suppose that the rabbi were to discover that the product is absolutely not kosher. What would he do about the thousands of items on grocery shelves? Would he recall them? With what authority? Indeed, one can only wonder whether a rabbi with such lax standards ever tried to recall a product that he discovered was not kosher.

[5] This statement makes it abundantly clear that the timing of the certification before the investigation cannot be explained as a carry-over from a previous year.

[6] We cannot find any reason that a rabbi who has not seen the process or even come to understand it from a phone call would consent to authorize a food producer to label a product as kosher. We feel, therefore, that only someone with very low standards of kashrus would trust any certification by this rabbi.

The K symbol does not always represent this sort of laxity. In fact, there are products labeled with a plain K that are of the highest standard. A prime example of this at this time is Kraft Products. Although Rabbi Levy, from the O/K, is actually the certifier of their K, the company often only allows a plain K to be placed on the label. Unfortunately, the K represents so many things that it represents nothing. The consumer would fare better relying on the several certification emblems on our symbol chart which can be found on page 18.

KASHRUS CONTRACT

Following is an example of a typical agreement between a reliable Kosher certifying agency and product manufacturer. This sample contract is for a company manufacturing kosher products only. Special situations where both kosher and non-kosher may be made in the same plant have more specific rules. In addition, anything involving the preparation of meat, poultry, fish or dairy products have specific contracts stipulating adherence to all the kosher laws involved in the preparation of these items.

AGREEMENT

This agreement made and entered into, in duplicate, this ____ day of ____, 19__, by and between the VAAD HAKASHRUS/ STAR-K KOSHER CERTIFICATION, a body corporate, party of the first part, sometimes hereafter referred to as the "COUNCIL", and ____, a body corporate, party of the second part, sometimes hereafter referred to as the "MERCHANT".

WITNESSETH

WHEREAS, the Council is a body duly incorporated for the purposes of kosher supervision within the Orthodox Jewish community, and ____.

WHEREAS, The Merchant hereby requests the Council to grant the Council's kosher supervision to products of the business enterprise known and operated by the Merchant, and ____.

WHEREAS, the Council is willing to grant the said supervision and issue certificates of kosher endorsement under the terms and conditions provided for hereafter,

AND WHEREAS, the Merchant hereby requests the Council to grant their Kashrus supervision to the ____ distributed from the following location:

IT IS THEREFORE AGREED BETWEEN THE PARTIES HERETO:

THAT the Vaad Hakashrus/Star-K Kosher Certification, hereby grants the requested supervision of the council under the following conditions:

14

1.   The Merchant agrees to abide by all requirements set forth by the Council regarding the production of kosher certified products. The Council shall be the sole authority and certifying agency as to the Kashrus (conformity with the Jewish Dietary Laws) of the above mentioned products.

2.   The Merchant agrees to produce all products kosher certified by the Council exclusively at plants acceptable to the Council.

3.   The Merchant agrees to forward all written inquiries concerning the kosher status of its products to the Council. However, copies of the kashrus certificate issued by the Council to the Merchant may be disseminated freely by the Merchant.

4.   The Merchant agrees to allow a representative of the council to enter all above-mentioned facilities of the Merchant during regular production hours in order to supervise the implementation of kosher-related regulations.

5.   The Merchant agrees to request approval from the Council for the use of any ingredients for kosher approved products made by the Merchant other than those previously approved by the Council.

6.   The printing of the Star-K on any label, container or package must be with the written approval of the Council. The Merchant agrees to notify the Council in advance of the printing order and the name and address of the printer.

7.   The Merchant agrees that the Star-K insignia and label are to be used only on those products endorsed by the Council.

8.   Upon request from the Council, the Merchant agrees to request from its supplier, a statement certifying that they will not change their formulas and/or raw materials used in kosher approved products without first notifying the council in advance.

9.   The Merchant agrees to request from its suppliers any information that may be required by the Council in ascertaining the Kashrus of approved kosher products.

10.   The Merchant agrees to request from its suppliers that the Council's representatives shall have the right to inspect those suppliers and processes at all times during regular business hours should such inspection be deemed necessary.

11.   All purchase invoices relevant to kosher certification shall be made available for inspection upon request by the Council.

12.   Upon request, the council shall have access to all formulas and manufacturing procedures used by the Merchant. However, the Merchant need not submit to the Council actual percentages of the individual components that he uses in the formulation of a product.

13.   The Merchant agrees that upon discontinuance of supervision by the Council, it will not label its products with the Star-K endorsement and will not advertise that its products are endorsed by the Council.

14.   The Merchant agrees that at the termination of this agreement all unused labels and containers bearing the Star-K be destroyed or obliterated under the supervision of the Council at no expense to the Council.

15.   In the event of any breach of the kashrus provisions of this agreement by the Merchant and so determined solely by the Council, the Council will notify the Merchant by registered mail that such a breach has occurred. It will then be up to the Council to determine whether its endorsement shall be withdrawn immediately or whether correction of the breach will be accepted. Should such a breach result in the immediate withdrawal of the Star-K endorsement, the Council reserves the right to notify the public through such media as it shall select, that the product or company is no longer supervised and endorsed by the Council. Under these circumstances, the Merchants shall be prohibited from using any form of the Council's endorsement as of the date of withdrawal of endorsement and any remaining unused containers, labels, or wrappers bearing the Council's endorsement shall be destroyed or the endorsement obliterated therefrom in the presence of a representative of the Council, within ten (10) days after such date. Nothing contained in this paragraph shall relieve the Merchant from paying the stipulated sum agreed to be paid to the council herein. The council shall not be held liable for any damage that the Merchant may incur as a result of such termination.

16.   The Council covenants and agrees that it will not communicate or divulge to, or use for the benefit of any other person, partnership, association, or corporation, any of the trade secrets, formulas, or secret processes used or employed by the Merchant in or about its business, that may be communicated to the Council by virtue of this licensing agreement.

17.   The Merchant agrees to pay the Council a ____ annual fee, for the first year that this agreement is in effect.

18.   This agreement shall run from ___ to ____ and shall unless either

16

party notifies the other by registered mail 45 days in advance of the expiration date. At the time of renewal the above mentioned supervisory fee shall be subject to review by the contracting parties.

19.   In the event that the Merchant changes its formulae to one which is not acceptable to the Council, or in the event that a supplier changes its formulae to one which will not be accepted by the Council, the Council shall withdraw its endorsement of that product. In such event, the Merchant shall be prohibited from using the labels which bear the Star-K for that product and the Council will have the right to notify the public of its termination of endorsement of that product through whichever media it sees fit. Labels not used bearing the Star-K endorsement of that product shall be destroyed as stated in Paragraph 15 above.

        IN WITNESS WHEREOF, the Parties hereto have executed this agreement by their corporate officers hereunto duly authorized:

COUNCIL_____   MERCHANT_____
Avrom Pollak, President
Star-K Kosher Certification
Vaad Hakashrus
7504 Seven Mile Lane
Baltimore, Maryland 21208
(410) 484-4110

SOME COMMON RELIABLE CERTIFICATION:

**ADAS YEREIM
OF VIENNER**

Rabbi Azriel Yehuda Lebovitz
27-31 Lee Ave., Brooklyn, NY 11211;
(718) 387-3680

**ADATH
YEREIM**

Rav Y.D. Frankfurter, Adath Yereim of Paris
10 Rue Cadet, 9e (Metro Cadet);
Tel. 42.46.36.47

AGUDAH

The Beth Din Zedek of Agudath Israel,
Moetzes Hakashrus, 2 Press St., Jerusalem,
POB 513;
Tel 02-385251-4

**BAIS DIN OF
CROWN HEIGHTS**

Bais Din of Crown Heights
788 Eastern Parkway, Room 212, Brooklyn,
N.Y. 11213;
Rabbi Dov Ber Levertov, Head Supervisor;
(718) 774-7504

BEDATZ

The Bais Din Tzedek of the Eida Hachareidis
of Jerusalem
Binyanei Zupnick 26A, Rechov Strauss, Jerusalem;
Tel. 02-251651 / 231084 FAX 02-254975
TELEFAX 972-2-254975

BELZ

The Bais Din Tzedek of K'hal Machzikei
Hadas
4 Sholel St., Jerusalem, Tel. 02-385832
4 Belza St., B'nai B'rak, Tel. 795414
FAX: 02-373884

THE "CHOF K"

Kosher Supervision Service
1444 Queen Ann Road, Teaneck, NJ 07666;
(201) 837-0500
Rabbi Aharon Felder, Director of Supervision.

**THE CALIFORNIA
"K"**

Kehilla Kosher
(Igud Hakashrus of L.A.)
186 N. Citrus,
Los Angeles, CA 90036
(213) 935-8383
Rabbi Avrohom Teichman,
Rabbinical Administrator.

**THE
"CHOF KOSHER"**

כשר

Rabbi Solomon B. Shapiro
73-09 136th Street, Flushing, NY 11367;
(718) 263-1574

THE "COR"

Kashruth Council - Orthodox Division
Toronto Jewish Congress,
4600 Bathhurst Street, Willowdale,
Ontario M2R 3V2;
(416) 635-9550
Rabbi M. Levin, Executive Director.

THE "cRc"

Chicago Rabbinical Council
3525 West Peterson Ave, Suite 315,
Chicago, IL 60659;
(312) 588-1600 • FAX (718) 384-6765
Rabbi Benjamin Shandalov,
Kashruth Administrator.

THE "CRC"

The Beth Din Hameyuchod L'inyonei
Kashruth of The Central Rabbinical Congress
(Hisachdus Horabonim),
85 Division Avenue, Brooklyn,
NY 11211;
(718) 384-6765 FAX: (718) 486-5574
Rabbi Yidel Gruber, Rabbinic Administrator.

THE "DIAMOND K"

Orthodox Vaad of Philadelphia
717 Callowhill Street, Philadelphia, PA 19123;
(215) 923-1216
Rabbinic Board: Rabbi Aaron Felder, Rabbi
Shlomo Caplan
and Rabbi Yehoshua Kagnaff.

THE "DK"

Vaad Hakahrus of Dallas, Inc.
(formerly Dallas Kashruth Council),
5530 Charlestown, Dallas, TX 75230;
(214) 934-VAAD (fax)
Rabbi David Shawl, Kashrus Administrator.

THE "DKC"

Dallas Kashruth Council, POB 30511, Dallas,
TX 75230;
73-09 136th Street, Flushing, NY 11367;
(214) 750-VAAD
Rabbi David Shawl, Rabbinic Administrator.

THE "GK"

Glatt Kosher – Nevei Achiezer
Shikun 6, Bnai Brak;
Rav Shlomo Mahpud, (03) 769-702,
Rav Baruch Roshgold, (03) 797-172.

Harabanut Harashit
58 King George Street,
Jerusalem, P.O.B. 7525, Tel. 247112

**THE HEART
K**

Kehila Kosher
186 North Citrus, Los Angeles, CA 90036;
(213) 935-8383
Rabbi Avromon Teichman, Rabbinic Administrator.

THE "IKS"

International Kosher Supervision-Corporate
3010 LBJ Freeway, Suite 905,
Dallas, TX 75234
(214) 247-1042, Fax: (214) 247-1050
Rabbi Chaim Perl, Rabbinic Administrator

THE "K-COR"

Vaad Harabonim of Greater Detroit and Merkaz
17071 West Ten Mile Road,
Southfield, MI 48075;
(313) 559-5005
Rabbi Beryl Broyde, Kashrus Administrator;
Rabbi Joseph Krupnik, Kashrus Director.

THE "KAJ"

Beth Din of K'hal Adath Jeshurun (Breuer's)
85-93 Bennett Avenue, New York, NY 10133;
(212) 923-3592, Harav Shimon Schwab,
Rosh Beth Din.

KEDASSIA

Kedassia, The Joint Kashrus Committee of
England
67 Amhurst Park, London, England.

THE "KSA"

Kosher Supervision of America
P.O. Box 35721
Los Angeles, CA 90035
(310) 282-0444, Fax (310) 282-0505
Rabbi Binyomin Lisbon, Kashrus Administrator

**THE LONDON
BETH DIN**

Court of the Chief Rabbi, Adler House
Tavistock Square, London WC1H 9HP,
England
Rabbi Berel Berkowitz, Registrar; 01-387-4300
FAX: 01-383-4934

THE "MK"

Montreal Vaad Hair
5491 Victoria Avenue, Montreal, Canada H3W 2PN;
(514) 739-6363 FAX: (514) 739-7024
Rabbi Niznik, Kashrus Director,
Rabbi Mordechai Tober, Kashrus Supervisor.

THE "MK"

Manchester Beth Din
435 Cheetam Hill Road, Manchester, 8, England;
Tel. 061-740-9711
Dayan O. Westheim, Rabbinic Administrator.

THE "NK"

National Kashruth
1 Route 306, Monsey, NY 10952;
(914) 352-4448 FAX: 914-356-9756
Rabbi Yacov Lipschutz, President;
Rabbi Mendel Simon, Administrator
Field Operations Barry Eizik, Director.

**THE OHIO
KASHRUS**

Ohio Kashruth
Rabbi Fant, Director of Supervision
6661 Meadowridge Lane, Cincinnati, OH 45237;
(513) 351-4140
Rabbi Chaim Edelstein, Rabbinic Administrator.

THE "O/K"

The Organized Kashrus Laboratories
1372 Carrol Street, Brooklyn, NY 11213;
(718) 756-7500
Rabbi Don Yoel Levy, Kashruth Administrator.

THE "O/U"

The Union of Orthodox Jewish Congregations
333 74th Ave. NY, NY 10001
(212) 563-4000
Rabbi Menachem Genack, Rabbinic Administrator

THE "OV"

Kosher Inspection Service of The Vaad Hoeir
of St. Louis
4 Millstone Campus, St. Louis, MO 63246;
(314) 569-2770
Rabbi Sholom Rivkin, Chief Rabbi.

Rabbi Zevulun Charlop
100 E. Mosholu Pkwy, Bronx, NY 10458
(212) 960-5344

Rabbi Yehoshua Heschel Deutsch (Freimaner Rav)
284 Keap St., Brooklyn, NY 11211;
(718) 782-1150

Rabbi Amram Feldman
Atlanta, LA

Rabbi Moshe Neuschloss
6 Truman Ave., New Square, NY 10977;
(914) 354-6563

Rabbi Michael Schick
San Francisco, CA
(415) 661-4055

Rabbi Moshe Stern (Debraciner Rav)
1514 49th St., Brooklyn, NY 11219;
(718) 851-5193

Rabbi Aaron Teitelbaum (Nirbater Rav)
1617 46th St., Brooklyn, NY 11204;
(718) 851-1221

Rabbi Nuchem Efraim (Noam) Teitelbaum
(Volver Rav); 5808 11th Ave., Brooklyn, NY 11219;
(718) 436-4685

Rav Chaim Yaakov Rottenberg
Chief Orthodoxe Rav of Paris (Grand Rabbin)
8 Rue Pavee, Paris-4;Tel. 48.87.49.03

Rabbi Asher Zeilingold
Kashrut Administrator of Upper Midwest Kashrut
1001 Prior Avenue South, St. Paul, MN 55116;
(612) 690-2137

THE "RCBC"

RCBC
(ועד הרבנים)

The Rabbinical Council of Bergen County
175 Van Nostrand Avenue, Englewood, NJ 07631;
Rabbi Meier Brueckheimer, Executive Director.

THE "RCC"

Community Kashrus Division of the Rabbinical
Council of California
1122 S. Robertson Blvd. Suite 8,
Los Angeles, CA 90035;
(310) 271-4160 FAX: (310) 271-7147
Rabbi Joshua Berkowitz, Chairman,
Rabbi Union, Rabbinic Administrator,
Rabbi Nissim Davidi, Kashrus Administrator
With Vaad of L.A. approval only.

Rabbinical Council of Orange County & Long Beach
5702 Clark Drive, Huntington Beach, CA 92649
(714) 846-2285, Kosher Hot Line (310) 426-4894

**THE
"SCROLL K"**

Vaad Hakashrus of Denver
1350 Vrain St, Denver, CO 80204;
(303) 595-9349
Rabbi Y. Feldberger, Rabbinic Administrator.

**THE "SEFER
TORAH-KASHER"** The Vaad Harabbonim of Flatbush
1618 Coney Island Avenue,
Brooklyn NY 11230;
(718) 951-8585
Rabbi Eli Skaist, Rabbinic Administrator.

THE "STAR K"

Vaad Hakashrus of the Orthodox Jewish
Council of Baltimore
11 Warren Road, Baltimore, MD
(410) 484-4110
Rabbi Moshe Heinemann, Rabbinic Administrator.

THE "TEXAS K"

Rabbi Perl,
POB 30662, Dallas, TX 75230

VAAD

Vaad HaKashrus of the Five Towns
859 Peninsula Blvd, Woodmere, NY 11598;
(516) 569-4536
Rabbi Moshe Chait, Kashrus Administrator.

VAAD HARABONIM
OF FLORIDA

Orthodox Rabbinical Council of South Florida
(Vaad Harabonim De Darom Florida)
3700 Sheridan Avenue, Miami Beach, FL 33140;
(305) 865-9851 673-0115;
Rabbi Tzvi Rosenbaum, Executive Secretary.

THE "VH"
THE "KVH"

Vaad Horabonim (Vaad Hakashrus) of
Massachusetts
177 Tremont Street, Boston, MA 02111
(617) 426-6268/2139
Rabbi Abraham Halbfinger, Rabbinic Administrator.

THE "VH"

Vaad Hoeir of Cincinnati
6446 Stover Avenue, Cincinnati, OH 45237;
(513) 731-4671
Rabbi Zelig Sharfstein, Rav;
Rabbi Joshua Goldman,
Rabbinic Administrator.

THE "VHCD"

Vaad Hakashruth of the Capital District
P.O. Box 9010, Albany, NY 12209;
(518) 489-1530
Rabbi Moshe Bomzer, Rav Hamachshir.
Rabbi Yaacov Kellman, Kashrus Administrator

THE "VHQ"

Vaad Harabonim of Queens
90-45 Myrtle Avenue, Glendale, NY 11385;
(719) 847-9206
Rabbi Shaul Chill, Chairman,
Kashruth Committee;
Executive Vice President, Rabbi Y.A.Sladowsky.

THE "VK"

Vancouver Kashruth
3476 Oak Street, Vancouver, B.C. V6H 2L8;
(604) 736-7607;
Rabbi Mordechai Fuerstein, Rabbinic Administrator.

THE "VHB"

The Vaad Hakashrus of Buffalo
P.O.B. 755, Williamsville, NY 14221;
(716) 634-3990
Rabbi Naphtali Burnstein, Rabbinic Administrator.

It is important to note, that these agencies frequently try to inform the consumer the full status of the products under their supervision. Following are some of their designations with their meanings.

D - Dairy
DE - Dairy Equipment (no actual dairy in ingredients, hence it can be eaten even after a meat meal)
P - Passover - Kosher for all year including Passover (Note: "P" <u>NEVER</u> designates pareve)
Pareve - Non-dairy
Cholov Yisroel - Kosher supervised milk used in ingredients
Pas Yisroel - Jewish baked foods
Yoshon - Not from current grain crop

27

SAMPLE OF KASHRUS CERTIFICATE:

STAR-K KOSHER CERTIFICATION
ORTHODOX JEWISH COUNCIL VAAD HAKASHRUS

7504 Seven Mile Lane / Baltimore, Maryland 21208-4531 / (301) 484-4110 / FAX (301) 653-9294

Bais-Din (Rabbinic Board)
RABBI YAAKOV KULEFSKY
RABBI MOSHE HEINEMANN
RABBI YAAKOV HOPPER

Rabbinic Administrator
RABBI MOSHE HEINEMANN

Director of Supervision
RABBI ELIYAHU SHUMAN

President
DR. AVROM POLLAK

January 3, 1991

White Wave, Inc.
6123 E. Arapahoe
Boulder, CO 80303

To whom it may concern:

    This is to certify that the following **Soy Products** manufactured by White Wave, Inc. of the above address are Kosher and Pareve for year round use, excluding Passover:

    This certification is valid until September 30, 1991 and is subject to renewal at that time.

Yours truly,

Eliyahu Shuman

Rabbi Eliyahu Shuman
Director of Supervision

RES:ek
8/25

A NON PROFIT AGENCY REPRESENTING THE KOSHER CONSUMER IN PROMOTING KASHRUS THROUGH EDUCATION, RESEARCH AND SUPERVISION

HISTORY OF KOSHER SUPERVISION

I n the U.S.A., the kosher certifying agencies with which we are familiar did not start until the 1920's and 1930's, but their development can be traced back over 200 years. The need for kosher supervision in the United States dates back to Colonial times. As early as 1660, a Jew from Portugal applied for a license to sell kosher meat in New Amsterdam. The first recorded complaint was in 1771 against the Shochet Moshe. In 1774, the widow, Hetty Hays, complained that her shochet (ritual slaughterer) was selling non-kosher meat. This led to the first court license revocation against a kosher butcher in 1796.

As Jewish communities developed in the United States, they originally followed the European pattern of having community appointed shochtim. By this method, the shochet could easily be removed if he did not follow the strict guidelines set down by the community leaders. This method changed drastically in 1813, when the schochet, Avraham Jacobs, became the first independent schochet in the United States. He was followed by many more. Unfortunately, this change led to a rapid decline in the standard of kosher meat.

In 1863, a group of laymen and shochtim got together to try to form a kashrus organization that could control this situation. Regrettably, they were unsuccessful. It was not until 1897 that the shochtim themselves banded together to form a union called "Meleches Hakodesh." Their goal was to improve kashrus standards, as well as the wages of shochtim.

By 1918, kosher products started finding their way into the American market. Abraham Goldstein, a chemist, was highly instrumental in both importing these products as well as in convincing domestic companies (such as Sunshine Biscuit Co.) to become certified kosher.

In 1924, the Union of Orthodox Rabbis (O/U), which had been established in 1892, decided to enter the field of kashrus. Mr. Goldstein was appointed as its first director. During the "food revolution" of the past 50 years, as more and more products are prepared in company plants and not in private kitchens, the "O/U" has been active as a non-profit organization in the kosher certification of these products.

Mr. Goldstein continued to head the O/U from 1924 until 1935. Feeling a need for another certifying agency, he started the O/K Laboratories. Today, the O/U, headed by Rabbi Menachem Genack, and the O/K, headed by Rabbi Don Yoel Levy, reliably certify many thousands of products and ingredients that we have become accustomed to using daily. As the complexity of manufacturing processes and the need for kosher certification has increased, so has the number of agencies and individuals interested in meeting this need. This has led to the rise of newer certifying agencies, such as VHM, the Chaf K, Kehilloh, Star K and others. Furthermore, individual rabbis have entered this field, often using their own kosher symbol or even just a plain "K" to designate a product's kosher status.

This has caused a great deal of confusion. When there were only two or three certifying agencies, it was easy for consumers to judge their reliability. But today, it may take a great deal of detective work to ascertain the standard that a particular rabbi is using. Consequently, many people prefer to rely on only the well-known certifying agencies, rather than risk the chance that a product may not meet their personal standard of kashrus.

KOSHER INFORMATION AGENCIES

Over the past few years, a few kosher information agencies have developed throughout the country. Some of these publish very useful guides with information on the latest developments in kashrus. These agencies are highly recommended. Of particular note is the publication from the **Kosher Information Bureau (KIB)** on the West Coast. They utilize a computer data base of over 100,000 to compile their newsletter and Passover Guide. Another highly acclaimed one is the **Kashrus Kurrents** from Baltimore. Listed here are some addresses for those wishing to subscribe to them:

Kosher Information Bureau
12753 Chandler Blvd., North Hollywood, CA 91607
(818) 762-3197, FAX (818) 980-6908

JFWS73A - Prodigy number
Rabbi E. Eidlitz, Rabbinic Administrator

Vaad Hakashrus of Baltimore - Kashrus Kurrents
7504 Seven Mile Lane, Baltimore, MD 21208
(410) 484-4110
Rabbi Moshe Heineman, Rabbinic Advisor

Kashrus Newsletter from Birkas Reuven
P.O. Box 204, Brooklyn, NY 11204
(718) 998-3201
Rabbi Yosef Wikler, Rabbinic Administrator

The Kosher Gram
Vaad Harabonim of Greater Detroit and Merkaz
17071 West Ten Mile Road
Southfield, MI 48075
(313) 559-5005
Rabbi Beryl Broyde, Kashrus Administrator
Rabbi Joseph Krupnik, Kashrus Director

FEDERAL AND STATE
KOSHER SLAUGHTER LAWS

O ver the years, many states have enacted various laws concerning "humane slaughter." Some of the details of these laws could be technically impossible to implement in kosher slaughter. Recognizing this problem, and wanting to satisfy the freedom-of-religion laws of the United States, most states have enacted special exemptions for Kosher Slaughter. Following are some prime examples of Federal and State laws concerning Kosher Slaughter.

United States Department of Agriculture
1989 Food and Agricultural Code

CHAPTER 6, SLAUGHTER

(Chapter 6 added by Stats. 1967, Ch. 1381)

19501. After June 1, 1968, cattle, calves, horses, mules, sheep, swine, or goats shall be slaughtered by the methods prescribed in this section. All state agencies shall contract for, purchase, procure, or sell all or any portion of only such animals as are slaughtered in conformity with the provisions of this chapter. The provisions of this chapter shall apply to any person engaged in the business of slaughtering animals enumerated in this section, or any person slaughtering any such animal when all or any part of such animal is subsequently sold or used for commercial purposes.

For the purposes of this section, prescribed methods are defined to be the following:

All cattle, calves, horses, mules, sheep, swine, or goats shall be either:

(a) Rendered insensible to pain by a captive bolt, gunshot, electrical or chemical means, or any other means that is rapid and effective before being cut, shackled, hoisted, thrown, or cast; or

(b) Handled, prepared for slaughter, and slaughtered in accordance with ritual requirements of the Jewish or any other religious faith that prescribes a method of slaughter whereby the animal suffers loss of consciousness by anemia of the brain caused by the simultaneous and instantaneous severance of the carotid arteries with a sharp instrument.

U.S. FEDERAL PUBLIC LAW 85-764

85th Congress, 2nd Session, H.R. 8308

August 27, 1958

LIVESTOCK — HUMANE METHODS OF SLAUGHTER

PUBLIC LAW 85-765; 72 STAT. 862.

[H.R. 8305]

An Act to establish the use of humane methods of slaughter of livestock as a policy of the United States, and for other purposes.

SEC. 2. No method of slaughtering or handling in connection with slaughtering shall be deemed to comply with the public policy of the United States unless it is humane. Either of the following two methods of slaughtering and handling are hereby found to be humane:

(a) In the case of cattle, calves, horses, mules, sheep, swine, and other livestock, all animals are rendered insensible to pain by a single blow or gunshot or an electrical, chemical or other means that is rapid and effective, before being shackled, hoisted, thrown, cast, or cut; or

(b) By slaughtering in accordance with the ritual requirements of the Jewish faith or any other religious faith that prescribes a method of slaughter whereby the animal suffers loss of consciousness by anemia of the brain caused by the simultaneous and instantaneous severance of the carotid arteries with a sharp instrument.

SEC. 6. Nothing in this Act shall be construed to prohibit, abridge, or in any way hinder the religious freedom of any person or group. Notwithstanding any other provision of this Act, in order to protect freedom of religion, ritual slaughter and the handling or other terms of this Act. For the purposes of this section the term "ritual slaughter" means slaughter in accordance with section 2 (b).

PUBLIC LAW 95-445 — OCT. 10, 1978

95th Congress

An Act

To amend the Federal Meat Inspection Act to require that meat inspected and approved under such Act be produced only from livestock slaughtered in accordance with humane methods, and for other purposes.

92 STAT. 1070

SEC. 6. Nothing in this Act shall be construed to prohibit, abridge, or in any way hinder the religious freedom of any person or group. Notwithstanding any other provision of this Act, in order to protect freedom of religion, ritual slaughter and the handling or other preparation of livestock for ritual slaughter are exempted from the terms of this Act. For the purposes of this section the term "ritual slaughter" means slaughter in accordance with section 2(b) of the Act of August 27, 1958 (72 U.S.C. 1902 (b.)

STATE OF WASHINGTON

Chapter 16.50 RCW

HUMANE SLAUGHTER OF LIVESTOCK

RCW 16.50.100 Declaration of policy

The legislature of the state of Washington finds that the use of humane methods in the slaughter of livestock prevents needless suffering; results in safer and better working conditions for persons engaged in the slaughtering industry; brings about improvement of products and economy in slaughtering operations; and produces other benefits for producers, processors and consumers which tend to expedite the orderly flow of livestock and their products. It is therefore declared to be the policy of the state of Washington to require that the slaughter of all livestock, and the handling of livestock in connection with slaughter, shall be carried out only by humane methods and to provide that methods of slaughter shall conform generally to those authorized by the Federal Humane Slaughter Act of 1958 and regulations thereunder. [1967 c 31 § 1]

RCW 16.50.150 Religious freedom — Ritual slaughter defined as humane. Nothing in this chapter shall be construed to prohibit, abridge, or in any way hinder the religious freedom of any person or group. Notwithstanding any other provisions of this chapter, ritual slaughter and the handling or other preparation of livestock for ritual slaughter is defined as humane. [1967 c 31 § 10]

STATE OF OREGON
Chapter 603
1981 REPLACEMENT PART, MEAT DEALERS AND SLAUGHTERERS
603.065 Slaughter methods. (1) Cattle, equines, sheep or swine shall be slaughtered by a licensee and handled in connection with slaughter, by any method which:

(a) Renders each such animal insensible to pain by a single blow or gunshot or by an electrical, chemical or other means that is rapid and effective, before the animal is shackled, hoisted, thrown, cast or cut; or

(b) Is in accordance with the ritual requirements of any religious faith that prescribes a method of slaughter whereby the animal suffers loss of consciousness by anemia of the brain caused by the simultaneous and instantaneous severance of the carotid arteries with a sharp instrument.

(2) No licensee engaged in the slaughter of animals described in subsection (1) of this section shall slaughter by any method other than therein described, nor shall shackle, hoist, or otherwise bring such animals not previously rendered insensible to pain in accordance with subsection (1) of this section into position for slaughter by any method which shall cause injury or pain. [1973 c.175 §48]

STATE OF MARYLAND
Article 27, § 331, HUMANE SLAUGHTER OF LIVESTOCK
§333A. Definitions

(a) As used in this subtitle these words are defined and shall be applied as follows:

(b) "Person" means any individual, partnership, corporation, or association doing business in this State, in whole or in part.

(c) "Slaughterer" means any person regularly engaged in the commercial slaughtering of livestock.

(d) "Livestock" means cattle, calves, sheep, swine, horses, mules, goats and any other animal which can or may be used in and for the preparation of meat or meat products, but does not include poultry or fowl.

(e) "Packer' means any person engaged in the business of slaughtering or of manufacturing or preparing meat or meat products for sale, either by such person or others; or of manufacturing or preparing livestock products for sale by such person or others.

(f) "Stockyard" means any place, establishment or facility commonly known as a stockyard, conducted or operated for compensation or profit as a public market, consisting of pens, or other enclosures, and their appurtenances, for the handling, keeping and holding of livestock for the purpose of sale or shipment.

(g) "Humane method" means either: (1) A method whereby the animal is rendered insensible to pain by mechanical, electrical, chemical or other means that is rapid and effective, before being shackled, hoisted, thrown, cast or cut; or (2) a method in accordance with ritual requirements of the Jewish faith or any other religious faith, whereby the animal suffers loss of consciousness by anemia of the brain caused by the simultaneous and instantaneous severance of the carotid arteries with a sharp instrument. The use of a manually operated hammer, sledge or poleax during slaughtering operations is specifically declared to be an inhumane method of slaughter within the meaning of this subtitle (1962, ch. 2)

§ 333B. Use of other than humane methods prohibited. No slaughterer, packer or stockyard operator shall shackle, hoist, or otherwise bring livestock into position for slaughter by any method other than a humane method. No slaughterer, packer, or stockyard operator shall bleed or slaughter any livestock except by a humane method. (1962, ch. 2)

§ 333C. Protection of freedom of religion; exemptions from subtitle. Nothing in this subtitle shall be construed to prohibit, abridge or in any way hinder the religious freedom of any person or group. Notwithstanding any other provision of this subtitle, in order to protect freedom of religion, ritual slaughter and the handling of other preparation of livestock for ritual slaughter are exempted from the terms of this subtitle. For the purposes of this section the term "ritual slaughter" means slaughter in accordance with §333A (g) (2). Nothing in this subtitle shall be construed to apply to a farmer while slaughtering his own livestock. (1962, ch. 2)

§14-902. False representation construed. A false representation prohibited by this subtitle includes: (1) Any oral or written statement that directly or indirectly tends to deceive or otherwise lead a reasonable individual to believe that a non-kosher product is kosher.

§14-903. False or misleading representations in sale of food products.

(a) A person may not sell or offer for sale any food that he falsely represents to be kosher or kosher for Passover.

(b) A person may not falsely represent any food or the contents of any package or container to be kosher or kosher for Passover by having or permitting to be inscribed on it, in any language, the words "kosher," "parve," or "glatt."

(c) (1) In this subsection, "Hebrew symbol" means

(i) Any Hebrew word or letter; or

(ii) Any symbol, emblem, sign, insignia, or other mark that simulates a Hebrew word or letter.

(2) In connection with any place of business that sells or offers for sale any food, a person may not display, whether in a window, door, or other location on or in the place of business, in any handbill or other printed matter distributed in or outside of the place of business, or otherwise in any advertisement, any Hebrew symbol unless he also displays in conjunction with the Hebrew symbol, in English letters of at least the same size as the characters used in the Hebrew symbol, the words "we sell kosher meat and food only," "we sell non-kosher meat and food only," or "we sell both kosher and non-kosher meat and food," as the appropriate case may be.

(d) (1) In this subsection, "fresh" means unprocessed other than by salting or soaking.

(2) A person may not sell or offer for sale, as kosher, any fresh meat or poultry unless the words "soaked and salted" or "not soaked and salted," as the appropriate case may be, is marked:

(i) On the package label; or

(ii) If the product is not packaged, on a sign prominently displayed in conjunction with the product.

(3) A person may not sell or offer for sale, as kosher, any fresh meat or poultry that is identified as "soaked and salted" unless the product has been soaked and salted in a manner which makes it kosher. (an. Code 1957, art. 27, § 196; 1975, ch. 49, § 3; 1979, ch. 536)

§14-907. Identification of packaged food products.

(a) In this section, "packaged food product" means a food product that:

(1) In advance of sale, is put up or packaged, in any manner, in units suitable

for retail sale; and

(2) Is not intended for consumption at its point of manufacture.

(b) A person may not sell or offer for sale, as kosher or kosher for Passover, any packaged food product unless:

(1) It has a kosher identification securely attached to the outside of the package; and

(2) This identification was attached to the package by the producer or packer of the product at his place of business.

(c) Subsection (b) applies to any packaged food product that is marked or identified with:

(1) In any language, the words "kosher," "parve," "glatt," "rabbinical supervision;"

(2) Any other word or symbol identifying the product as kosher or kosher for Passover; or

(3) The English letters "K" "KP," "KD," "KM," "KF," "KOS," or "RS," except as part of a registered trademark. (1979, ch. 536)

County Sec. 18-12. Kosher foods.

(a) (1) The word "person," when used in this section, shall include association, firm, partnership, corporation or agent or employee of any thereof.

(2) The word "kosher," when used in this section, shall mean sanctioned by Jewish law, that is to say prepared under or consisting of a product or products sanctioned by the Orthodox Hebrew religious rules and requirements and dietary laws as defined in "Shulchan Aruch," "Yoreh Deah" and "Oruch Chaim," and as construed and interpreted from time to time by the Council of Orthodox Rabbis of Baltimore.

(3) The word "food," when used in this section, shall include the following for human consumption on or off premises: Meat, meat products, meat preparations, food, food products, food preparations and beverages, both alcoholic and non-alcoholic.

(b) Any person who, with intent to defraud, serves, sells or exposes for sale in any hotel, inn, restaurant, boarding house, lunchroom, caterer, grocer and all other places where food is served or sold for human consumption, on or off the premises, and falsely represents same to be kosher, either by direct or indirect statements, orally or in writing, which might reasonably be calculated to deceive or lead a reasonable man to believe that a representation is being made that such food is kosher, shall be guilty of a misdemeanor.

(c) Any person who, in any place where food is served or sold for human consumption, displays on his window, door or in his place of business or in handbills or other printed matter or advertisement, distributed in or outside his premises, words or letters in Hebraic or other characters, or any sign, emblem, insignia, six point star, symbol or marking simulation of same without displaying in conjunction therewith in English letters of at least the same size as such characters, signs, emblems, insignia, symbols or marks, the words "We Sell Kosher Food Only" or "We Sell Non-Kosher Food Only" or "We Sell Both Kosher and Non-Kosher Foods," as the case may be, shall be guilty of a misdemeanor.

(d) Mere possession of non-kosher food in any place of business advertising the serving or sale of kosher food only, is presumptive evidence that the person in possession of such food exposes the same for serving and/or for sale, with intent to defraud, in violation of the provisions of this section.

(e) In order to comply with the provisions of this section, persons serving and selling or exposing for sale kosher foods only, or both kosher and non-kosher foods, must adhere to and abide by Orthodox Hebrew religious rules and requirements and the dietary laws as defined in "Shulchan Aruch," "Yoreh Deah" and "Oruch Chaim;" otherwise they shall be in violation of this section.

(f) Any person engaged in the manufacture, sale, preparation or distribution of any kosher foods, whether the same be raw or cooked, who shall willfully refuse to permit the inspector to enter upon or in their premises for the purpose of carrying out his duties as outlined under subsection of this section, and/or who shall willfully interfere with the said inspector's performance of his duties as outlined in subsection (h) of this section, shall be guilty of a misdemeanor.

Baltimore City Regulations 49 : KOSHER MEAT

(a) *Bureau.* There is hereby established a Bureau to be designated and known as the "Bureau of Kosher Meat and Food Control," and for the proper conduct of said Bureau and for the purpose hereinafter set forth the Mayor shall appoint six (6) persons qualified as hereinafter provided. The Bureau shall consist of three (3) duly ordained orthodox Rabbis and three (3) laymen selected from a list to be submitted by "The Council of Orthodox Rabbis of Baltimore" and "The Orthodox Jewish Council of Baltimore."

The members of the Bureau of Kosher Meat and Food Control shall receive no compensation for their services hereunder.

(b) *Appointees.* Appointees shall be of high standing for their expert knowledge and interest in the orthodox Hebrew rules, regulations and requirements pertaining to the sale, manufacture, distribution and preparation of kosher meat, meat preparations, food and food products for human consumption on or off premises.

And the appointees shall be persons whose capacity for such expert knowledge is generally recognized in the community and shall be persons who are not financially interested in the manufacture, sale or distribution of any such products.

50. Sales to defraud.

Any person, firm or corporation who, with intent to defraud, sells, exposes for sale, any meat or meat preparation, article of food or food products, and falsely represents the same to be Kosher, whether such meat or meat preparation, article of food or food product be raw or prepared for human consumption, or as having been prepared under and/or of a product or products sanctioned by the orthodox Hebrew religious rules and requirements or under the dietary laws either by direct or indirect statement, orally or serves, sells or exposes for sale in any hotel, inn, restaurant, boarding house, eating house, lunch room, caterers or grocers or other place where food products or food are sold for human consumption on or off the premises, any meat preparation food or food product, and falsely represents the same to be kosher, whether such meat, meat preparation, food or food product be raw or prepared, or as having been prepared under and/or of a product or products sanctioned by the orthodox Hebrew religious rules or requirements and/or dietary laws, either by direct or indirect statement, orally or in writing, which might reasonably be calculated to deceive or lead a reasonable man to believe that a representation is being made that such food is kosher or prepared in accordance with the orthodox Hebrew religious rules or requirements and/or dietary laws, or falsely represents any food product or the contents of any package or containers to be so constituted and prepared, by having or permitting to be inscribed thereon the word "Kosher" in any language; or sells or exposes for sale in the same place of business both kosher and non-kosher meat preparations, food or food products, either raw or prepared, and who fails to indicate on his window signs and all display signs and advertising in block letters of at least four inches in height "Kosher and Non-Kosher Food Sold Here," and who exposes for sale in any show window or place of business or who serves food off the premises both kosher and non-kosher food or food products, either raw or prepared, and who fails to display over each kind of food or food preparation a sign in block letters of at least four inches in height reading "Kosher Food" or "Non-Kosher Food," as the business, or in hand bills or other printed matter or advertisement distributed in any manner or way, words or letters in Hebraic or other characters, or any sign, emblem, insignia, six pointed star, symbol or mark in simulation of same without displaying in conjunction therewith in English letters of at least the same size the words "We Sell Kosher Food Only," or "We Sell Non-Kosher Food Only," or "We Sell Both Kosher and Non-Kosher Food," as the case may be, is guilty of a misdemeanor.

STATE OF RHODE ISLAND
Chapter 17
HUMANE SLAUGHTER OF LIVESTOCK

4-17-2. Definitions — As used in chapter:

(a) "Director" means the director of environmental management.

(b) "Person" means any individual, partnership, corporation, or association doing business in this state, in whole or in part.

(c) "Slaughterer" means any person who regularly engages in the commercial slaughtering of livestock.

(d) "Livestock" means cattle, cows, sheep, swine, horses, mules, goats and any other animal which can or may be used in and for the preparation of meat or meat products.

(e) "Packer" means any person engaged in the business of slaughtering or manufacturing or preparing meat or meat products for sale, either by that person or others; or of manufacturing or preparing livestock products for sale by that person or others.

(f) "Stockyard" means any place, establishment, or facility commonly known as a stockyard, conducted or operated for compensation or profit as a public market, consisting of pens, or other enclosures, and their appurtenances, for the handling, keeping and holding of livestock for the purpose of sale or shipment.

(g) "Humane method" means either:

(1) A method whereby the animal is rendered insensible to pain by mechanical, electrical, chemical or other means that is rapid and effective before being shackled, hoisted, thrown, cast or cut; or

(2) A method in accordance with the ritual requirements of the Jewish faith or any other religious faith whereby the animal suffers loss of consciousness by anemia of the brain caused by the simultaneous and instantaneous severance of the carotid arteries with a sharp instrument.

4-17-7. Penalty for violations. — Nothing in this chapter shall be construed to prohibit, abridge, or in any way hinder the religious freedom of any person or group. Notwithstanding any other provision of this chapter, in order to protect freedom of religion, ritual slaughter and the handling or other preparation of livestock for ritual slaughter are exempted from the terms of this chapter. For the purpose of this section, the term "ritual slaughter" means slaughter in accordance with § 4-172(g)(2).

STATE OF ARIZONA
ARIZONA REVISED STATUTES, ARIZONA DEPARTMENT OF AGRICUL-TURE
3-2016. Methods of slaughtering which are humane
(Eff. 1/1/91).

No method of slaughtering or handling in connection with slaughtering shall be deemed to comply with the public policy of the state of Arizona unless it is humane. Either of the following two methods of slaughtering and handling are hereby found to be humane:

1. In the case of cattle, calves, horses, mules, sheep, swine, and other livestock, all animals are rendered insensible to pain by a single blow or gunshot or an electrical, chemical or other means that is rapid and effective, before being shackled, hoisted, thrown, cast, or cut.

2. By slaughtering in accordance with the ritual requirements of the Jewish faith or any other religious faith that prescribes a method of slaughter whereby the animal suffers loss of consciousness by anemia of the brain caused by the simultaneous and instantaneous severance of the carotid arteries with a sharp instrument.

STATE OF CALIFORNIA

Bill Number: AB 887

THE PEOPLE OF THE STATE OF CALIFORNIA DO ENACT AS FOLLOWS: SECTION 1. Section 12024.12 is added to the Business and Professions Code, to read:

12024.12 (a) Any person who sells fresh meat or poultry advertised or represented to be kosher shall retain for one year a true and legible copy of all invoices and records of cash or charge transactions from the packer or producer of the kosher meat or poultry and shall make these documents, and other evidence of the source of the meat being housed or sold by that person, available for inspection by the Department of Food and Agriculture or its representatives, upon request.

(b) Notwithstanding any other provision of law, the Director of Food and Agriculture shall enforce this section, as a pilot program in Los Angeles County until January 1, 1987, if adequate funding, as determined by the director, is made available.

(c) This section shall remain in effect only until January 1, 1987, and as of that date is repealed, unless a later enacted statute, which is chaptered before January 1, 1987, deletes or extends that date.

BILL TEXT

SEC. 2. The sum of forty-six thousand dollars ($46,000) is hereby appropriated from the General Fund to the Department of Food and Agriculture to carry out its duties pursuant to Section 12024.12 of the Business and Professions Code.

SEC. 3. No reimbursement is required by this act pursuant to Section 6 of Article XIIIB of the California Constitution because the only cost which may be incurred by a local agency or school district will be incurred because this act creates a new crime or infraction, changes the definition of a crime or infraction, changes the penalty for a crime or infraction, or eliminates a crime or infraction.

SEC. 4. This act is an urgency statute necessary for the immediate preservation of the public peace, health, or safety within the meaning of Article IV of the Constitution and shall go into immediate effect. The facts constituting the necessity are:

In order to ensure that consumers of fresh kosher meat and poultry will be adequately protected in their choice of that product and can have confidence in the state's ensuring the reliability of that product, it is necessary that this act take effect immediately.

KOSHER LAWS
FROM CALIFORNIA STATE PENAL CODE

§383b. Kosher meats and meat preparations; sale and labeling regulations; false representations; punishment; kosher defined

Every person who with intent to defraud, sells or exposes for sale any meat or meat preparations, and falsely represents the same to be kosher, whether such meat or meat preparations be raw or prepared for human consumption, or as having been prepared under and from a product or products sanctioned by the orthodox Hebrew religious requirements; or falsely represents any food product, or the contents of any package or container, to be so constituted and prepared, by having or permitting to be inscribed thereon the words "kosher" in any language; or sells or exposes for sale in the same place of business both kosher and non-kosher meat or meat preparations, either are prepared for human consumption, who fails to indicate on his window signs in all display advertising in block letters at least four inches in height "kosher and non-kosher meats sold here" or who exposes for sale in any show window or place of business as both kosher and non-kosher meat preparations, either raw or prepared for human consumption, who fails to display over each kind of meat or meat preparation so exposed a sign in block letters at least four inches in height, reading "kosher meat" or "non-kosher meat" as the case may be; or sells or exposes for sale in any restaurant or any other place where food products are sold for consumption on the premises, any article of food or food preparations and falsely represents the same to be kosher, or as having been prepared in accordance with the orthodox Hebrew religious requirements; or sells or exposes for sale in such restaurant, or such other place, both kosher and non-kosher food or food preparations for consumption on the premises, not prepared in accordance with the Jewish ritual, or not sanctioned by the Hebrew orthodox religious requirements, and who fails to display on his window signs in all display advertising, in block letters at least four inches in height "kosher and non-kosher food served here" is guilty of a misdemeanor and upon conviction thereof be punishable by a fine of not less than one hundred dollars ($100), nor more than six hundred dollars ($600) or imprisonment in the county jail of not less than 30 days, nor more than 90 days, or both such fine and imprisonment.

45

The word "kosher" is here defined to mean a strict compliance with every Jewish law and custom pertaining and relating to the killing of the animal or fowl from which the meat is taken or extracted, the dressing, treatment and preparation thereof for human consumption, and the manufacture, production, treatment and preparation of such other food or foods in connection wherewith Jewish laws and customs obtain and to the use of tools, implements, vessels, utensils, dishes and containers that are used in connection with the killing of such animals and fowling the dressing preparation, production manufacture and treatment of such meats and other products, foods and food stuffs.

(Added by Stats. 1931, c. 1029, p. 2147, § 1. Amended by Stats. 1983, c. 1092,§ 278, urgency, eff. Sept. 27, 1983, operative Jan. 1, 1984.)

Historical Note

The 1983 amendment increased the minimum fine from $50 to $100; increased the maximum fine from $300 to $600; and made non-substantive changes.

Cross References

Enforcement, see Health and Safety Code, § 214.

Library References

Food–7,15.
C.J.S. Food § 12(8) et seq.
rds and Phrases (Perm. Ed.)

WESTLAW Electronic Research

See WESTLAW Electronic Research guide following the Preface.

Notes of Decisions

Compliance with Jewish law and custom[2] Kosher style[3] Validity[1]

1. Validity

This section proscribing selling meat, misrepresenting it to be kosher, requires specific intent to defraud, and, in view thereof, is not void for vagueness. Erlich v. Municipal Court of Beverly Hills Judicial Dist. (1961) 11 Cal. Rptr. 758, 360 P.2d 334, 55 C.2d 553.

2. Compliance with Jewish law and custom

This section proscribing fraudulently misrepresenting meat as kosher and defining kosher to mean strict compliance with every Jewish law and pertinent custom is limited to such laws and customs as are generally recognized among orthodox Hebrew religious requirements. Erlich v. Municipal Court of Beverly Hills Judicial Dist (1961) 11 Cal. Rptr. 758, 360 P.2d 334, 55 C.2d 553.

3. Kosher style

Food processors who pack dill pickles and label them "kosher style" when such pickles are not prepared and packed in such a manner as to render them strictly kosher according to orthodox Jewish ritual requirements do not violate this section. 30 Ops. Atty. Gen. 312.

§101.29 Labeling of kosher and kosher style foods.

The term "kosher" should be used only on food products that meet certain religious dietary requirements. The precise significance of the phrase "kosher style" as applied to any particular product by the public has not been determined. There is a likelihood that the use of the term may cause the prospective purchaser to think that the product is "kosher." Accordingly, the Food and Drug Administration believes that use of the phrase should be discouraged on products that do not meet the religious dietary requirements.

California Senate Bill No. 1864
Chapter 990

An act to amend Section 12024.12 of the Business and Professions Code, relating to kosher food, making an appropriation therefore, and declaring the urgency thereof, to take effect immediately.
(Approved by the Governor, September 19, 1988. Filed with Secretary of State, September 20, 1988.)

LEGISLATIVE COUNSEL'S DIGEST

SB 1864, Rosenthal. Kosher food.

(1) Existing law requires, until July 1, 1988, that any person who sells fresh meat or poultry advertised or represented to be kosher retain specified records from the packer or producer of the meat or poultry for one

year and to make these records available for inspection by the Department of Food and Agriculture. Violation of these provisions is a misdemeanor. The Director of Food and Agriculture is required to enforce these requirements in the Counties of Alameda, Los Angeles, Orange, San Diego, and Santa Clara and the City and County of San Francisco as a pilot program until July 1, 1988, if adequate funding is available.

This bill would extend the July 1, 1988 termination date for these provisions to January 1, 1994, thus imposing a state-mandated local program by continuing the existence of a misdemeanor. The bill would also require the department to evaluate the effectiveness of this program, as specified, and to report this evaluation to the Legislature by January 1, 1994.

(2) The California Constitution requires the state to reimburse local agencies and school districts for certain costs mandated by the state. Statutory provisions establish procedures for making that reimbursement.

This bill would provide that no reimbursement is required by this act for a specified reason.

(3) The bill would appropriate $70,000 to the department to carry out the program.

(4) The bill would declare that it is to take effect immediately as an urgency statute.

Appropriation: yes.

The people of the State of California do enact as follows:

SEC. 1. Section 12024.12 of the Business and Professions Code is amended to read:

12024.12 (a) Any person who sells fresh meat or poultry advertised or represented to be kosher shall retain, on the premises, for one year, a true and legible copy of all invoices and records of cash or charge transactions from the packer or producer of the kosher meat or poultry and shall make these documents, and other evidence of the source of the meat being housed or sold by that person, available for inspection by the Department of Food and Agriculture or its representatives, upon request.

(b) Notwithstanding any other provision of law, the Director of Food and Agriculture shall enforce this section, as a pilot program in the Counties of Alameda, Los Angeles, Orange, San Diego, and Santa Clara and the City and County of San Francisco if adequate funding, as determined by the director, is made available.

(c) This section shall remain in effect only until January 1, 1994, and as of that date is repealed, unless a later enacted statute, which is enacted before January 1, 1994, deletes or extends that date.

SEC. 2 The Department of Food and Agriculture shall evaluate the effectiveness of the pilot program conducted pursuant to Section 12024.12 of the Business and Professions Code, and shall report to the Legislature on its effectiveness by January 1, 1994. The effectiveness of the pilot program shall be demonstrated by a reduction of not less than 75 percent in allegations of fraudulent kosher meat products made to the Attorney General and to appropriate consumer agencies since the program's inception on August 1, 1985. The evaluation shall include a determination of the cost effectiveness of the pilot program and recommendations regarding whether it should be continued, reduced, expanded, or modified. The department shall use not more than 7 percent of the program's final year appropriation for purposes of preparing the report to the Legislature.

SEC. 3. No reimbursement is required by this act pursuant to Section 6 of Article XIII B of the California Constitution because the only cost which may be incurred by a local agency or school district will be incurred because this act creates a new crime or infraction, changes the definition of a crime or infraction, changes the penalty for a crime or infraction, or eliminates a crime or infraction.

SEC. 4. The sum of seventy thousand dollars ($70,000) is hereby appropriated from the General Fund to the Department of Food and Agriculture to carry out Section 12024.12 of the Business and Professions Code.

SEC 5. This act is an urgency statute necessary for the immediate preservation of the public peace, health, or safety within the meaning of Article IV of the Constitution and shall go into immediate effect. The facts constituting the necessity are:

In order to ensure a continuing supply of genuine, high-quality kosher meat in this state, it is necessary that this act take effect immediately.

KOSHER LAWS
FROM NEW YORK STATE PENAL CODE

Provisions of Agriculture and Markets Law
Relating to SALE OF KOSHER MEAT AND FOODS
With Rules and Regulations
Revised January 1988 (Includes amendments through the 1987 legislative session)

PROVISIONS OF AGRICULTURE AND MARKETS LAW IN
RELATION TO KOSHER LAW ENFORCEMENT

Article 2
Section 16. General powers and duties of department.

The department through the commissioner shall have power to: Investigate, inspect and supervise the sale and exposure for sale of meat and meat preparations and enforce the provisions of sections two hundred one-a, two hundred one-b and two hundred one-c of this chapter relating thereto, designate an employee of the department as "director of kosher law enforcement" and to make such rules and regulations imposing such additional requirements and restrictions upon such sale and exposure for sale as may be deemed necessary in connection with or in aid of the proper administration and enforcement of such provisions and of any other applicable laws.

26-a Advisory board on kosher law enforcement.

1. There is hereby established in the department an advisory board on kosher law enforcement which shall consist of nine members, to be appointed by the commissioner of the department of agriculture and markets. Of the members first appointed, three shall be appointed for terms of one year, three for terms of two years and three for terms of three years. Their successors shall be appointed for terms of three years. The commissioner shall designate one of such appointees to be chairman of the advisory board. The advisory board may elect from its membership, a vice-chairman and a secretary. Vacancies

in the membership of the advisory board occurring from any cause, shall be filled by the commissioner for the unexpired term.

2. The commissioner may detail from time to time to the assistance of the advisory board such employees of the department as may be required, and shall provide suitable space in the office of the department for the meetings and records of the advisory board.

3. The advisory board shall meet at the call of the commissioner and at such other times as it may deem necessary and at such places as may be convenient.

4. It shall be the duty of the advisory board hereby established to advise, counsel and confer with the commissioner on matters of policy in connection with the administration and enforcement of laws and rules relating to kosher meats, meat preparations, and food products to consider all matters submitted to it by the commissioner, and on its own initiative to recommend to the commissioner such changes in the laws or rules relating to the possession, sale and exposure for sale of kosher meats, meat preparations, and food products, as may be deemed advisable to secure the effective administration and enforcement of such laws and rules and, with the consent of the commissioner, to submit for enactment by the legislature such draft or drafts of legislation imposing such further restrictions on the possession, sale and exposure for sale of kosher meats, meat preparations and food products, as may be deemed necessary.

5 . The advisory board shall adopt rules and regulations to govern its own proceedings. The secretary shall keep a complete record of all its proceedings which shall show the names of the members present at each meeting and any action taken by the advisory board. The record shall be filed in the office of the department. All records and other documents of the department relating to matters within the jurisdiction of the advisory board shall be subject to inspection by members of the advisory board.

6. The members of the advisory board shall receive no compensation for their services hereunder, but they shall be entitled to reimbursement for their actual and necessary traveling and other expenses heretofore or hereafter incurred by them in connection with the performance of their duties under this section.

Article 17

201-a. Sale Or kosher meat and meat preparations, kosher articles of food and food products.

l. A person who, with intent to defraud, sells or exposes for sale any meat or meat preparations, article of food or food products, and falsely represents the same to be kosher or kosher for Passover, whether such meat or meat preparations, article of food or food products, be raw or prepared for human consumption, or as having been prepared under, and of a product or products sanctioned by, the orthodox Hebrew religious requirements, either by direct statement orally, or in writing, which might reasonably be calculated to deceive or lead a reasonable man to believe that a representation is being made that such food is kosher or prepared in accordance with the orthodox Hebrew religious requirements, or falsely represents any food

products or the contents of any package or container to be so constituted and prepared, by having or permitting to be inscribed thereon the word "kosher" or "kosher-style" in any language; or sells or exposes for sale a non-kosher meat or meat preparation, or food or food product, which is labeled or advertised with the words "Jewish" or "Hebrew", either alone or in conjunction with the words "style" or "type" or any similar expression, unless the word "non-kosher" is displayed in English letters, of at least the same size as the words "Jewish" or "Hebrew", either alone or in conjunction with the words "style" or "type" or any similar expression; or sells or exposes for sale in the same place of business both kosher and non-kosher meat or meat preparations, or both kosher and non-kosher food or food products, either raw or prepared for human consumption, and who fails to indicate on his window signs and all display advertising, in block letters at least four inches in height, "kosher and non-kosher meat sold here", or "kosher and non-kosher food sold here", or who exposes for sale in any show window or place of business both kosher and non-kosher meat or meat preparations, or kosher and non-kosher food or food products, either raw or prepared for human consumption, and who fails to display over each kind of meat or meat preparation so exposed a sign in block letters at least four inches in height reading "kosher meat", or "non-kosher meat", as the case may be, or "kosher food" or "non-kosher food", as the case may be, or who displays on his window, door, or in his place of business, or in hand-bills or other printed

52

matter distributed in or outside of his place of business, words or letters in Hebraic characters other than the word "kosher", or any sign, emblem, insignia, six-pointed star, symbol, or mark in simulation of same, without displaying in conjunction therewith in English letters of at least the same size as such characters, signs, emblems, insignia, symbols, or marks, the words "we sell kosher meat and food only", or "we sell non-kosher meat and food only", or "we sell both kosher and non-kosher meat and food", as the case maybe, is guilty of a class A misdemeanor, except that a person who with intent to defraud sells or exposes for sale on premises any meat or meat preparations and falsely represents the same to be kosher or kosher for Passover, provided said meat or meat preparations in violation has a retail value in excess of five thousand dollars, whether such meat or meat preparations be raw or prepared for human consumption, is guilty of a class E felon. Possession of non-kosher meat and food, in any place of business advertising the sale of kosher meat and food only, is presumptive evidence that the person in possession exposes the same for sale with intent to defraud, in violation of the provisions of this section

2. All fresh meats and poultry offered for sale at retail as kosher shall be marked on the label when packaged or by a sign when not packaged, with the words "soaked and salted" or "not soaked and salted" as the case maybe. Such words when marked on the label or by a sign shall be in letters at least as large as the letters of the words on the label or sign designating such meat and poultry as kosher.

3. Fresh meat and poultry shall be defined as meat that has not been processed except for salting and soaking.

201-b. Sale of kosher meat and food in hotels and restaurants

1. A person who, with intent to defraud, sells or exposes for sale in any hotel, restaurant, or other place where food products are sold for consumption on or off the premises, any meat or meat preparations, article of food or food products, and falsely represents the same to be kosher or kosher for Passover, whether such meat or meat preparations, article of food or food products be raw or prepared for human consumption, or as having been prepared under, and of a product or products sanctioned by, the orthodox Hebrew religious requirements, either by direct statement orally, or in

writing, which might reasonably be calculated to deceive or lead a reasonable man to believe that a representation is being made that such food is kosher or prepared in accordance with the orthodox Hebrew religious requirements, or falsely represents any food product or the contents of any package or container to be so constituted and prepared, by having or permitting to be inscribed thereon the word "kosher" or "kosher-style" in any language; or sells or exposes for sale a non-kosher meat or meat preparation, or food or food product, which is labeled or advertised with the words "Jewish" or "Hebrew", either alone or in conjunction with the words "style" or "type" or any similar expression, unless the word "non-kosher" is displayed in English letters, of at least the same size as the words "Jewish" or "Hebrew", either alone or in conjunction with the words "style" or "type" or any similar expression; or sells or exposes for sale in the same place of business both kosher and non-kosher meat or meat preparations or both kosher and non-kosher food or food products, either raw or prepared for human consumption, and who fails to indicate on his window signs and all display advertising, in block letters at least four inches in height, "kosher and non-kosher food sold here", or who exposes for sale in any show window or place of business both kosher and non-kosher food or food products, either raw or prepared for human consumption, and who fails to display over each kind of food or food preparation so exposed a sign in block letters at least four inches in height reading "kosher food" or "non-kosher food", as the case may be, or who displays on his window, door, or in his place of business, or in handbills or other printed matter distributed in or outside of his place of business, words or letters in Hebraic characters other than the word "kosher", or any sign, emblem, insignia, six-pointed star, symbol, or mark in simulation of same, without displaying in conjunction therewith in English letters of a least the same size as such characters, signs, emblems, insignia, symbols, or marks the words "We sell kosher food only," or "We sell non-kosher food only," or "We sell both kosher and non-kosher food", as the case may be, is guilty of a misdemeanor, except that a person who with intent to defraud sells or exposes for sale on premises any meat or meat preparations and falsely represents the same to be kosher or kosher for Passover, provided said meat or meat preparations in violation has a retail value in excess of five thousand dollars, whether such meat or meat preparations be raw or prepared for human consumption, is guilty of a class E felony. Possession of non-kosher food, in any place of business advertising the sale of kosher food only, is presumptive evidence that the person in possession exposes the same for sale with intent to defraud, in violation of the provisions of this section. 2. Any food establishment or caterer that offers for sale, food prepared on the premises which is represented as kosher, shall file with the department the name and address of the supervising Rabbi or certifying organization or the name and address of the person under whose supervision said food products have been prepared as kosher. Food establishments that fail to file with the department the name and address of the supervising Rabbi or certifying organization or the name and address of the person under whose supervision said food products have been prepared as kosher shall be liable to a civil fine not to exceed one hundred dollars.

201-c. Fraudulent identification of food and food products. No person shall:

1 . Wilfully mark, stamp, tag, brand, label or in any other way or by any other means of identification, represent or cause to be marked, stamped, tagged, branded, labeled or represented as kosher or kosher style or as having been prepared in accordance with the Hebrew orthodox religious requirements food or food products not kosher or not so prepared, or
2. Wilfully remove, deface, obliterate, cover, alter, or destroy or cause to be removed, defaced, obliterated, covered, altered or destroyed the original slaughter-house plumba or any other mark, stamp, tag, brand, label or any other means of identification affixed to foods or food products to indicate that such foods or food products are kosher or have been prepared in accordance with the Hebrew orthodox religious requirements, or
3. Knowingly sell, dispose of or have in his possession, for the purpose of resale to any person as kosher, any food or food products not having affixed thereto the original slaughter-house plumba or any other mark, stamp, tag, brand, label or other means of identification employed to indicate that such food or food products are kosher or have been prepared in accordance with the Hebrew orthodox religious requirements or any food or food products to which such plumba, mark, stamp, tag, brand, label or other means of identification has or have been fraudulently affixed.

201-d. Violations and penalties.

Any violation of any of the provisions of section two hundred one-a, two hundred one-b, two hundred one-c or two hundred one-e of this chapter shall be a class A misdemeanor, except that a person who with intent to defraud sells or exposes for sale on premises any meat or meat preparations and falsely represents the same to be kosher or kosher for Passover, provided said meat or meat preparations in violation has a retail value in excess of five thousand dollars, whether such meat or meat preparations be raw or prepared for human consumption, is guilty of a class E felony. Where any person has previously been convicted of a violation of section two hundred one-a, two hundred one-b, or two hundred one-c of this chapter within the preceding ten years, upon conviction for a second or subsequent violation such person may be fined up to ten thousand dollars in addition to any other penalties provided by law.

201-e. Kosher and kosher for Passover identification.

1. All articles of food or food products, both liquid and solid, sold as kosher or kosher for Passover in any container shall have a kosher or kosher for Passover identification securely affixed on the outside of such container only by the manufacturer or packer at his premises. No person other than such manufacturer or packer shall possess or affix such marks of identification.

2. All articles of food or food products, which are not packaged in a container and are sold as kosher or kosher for Passover shall have a kosher or kosher for Passover identification securely affixed thereto by the manufacturer at his premises. No person other than such manufacturer or packer shall possess or affix such marks of identification.

2-a. In the event that non-prepackaged fresh meat or poultry is sold and delivered off-premises as Kosher the meat or poultry and the bill of sale, if any, rendered at the time of delivery shall have affixed to them a label or the printed words "not soaked and salted" or "soaked and salted" as the case may be.

3. Any food commodity in package form which is certified by an organization, identified by any symbol or is marked as being kosher for Passover shall not be offered for sale by the producer or distributor of such food

commodity until thirty days after such certifying organization, producer or distributor shall have registered the name, current address and telephone number of the supervising rabbi with the department.

3-a. Any food commodity in package form which is marked "rabbinical supervision" or marked with a "k", "km", "kos" or "kp" except a registered trademark shall not be offered for sale by the producer or distributor of such food commodity until thirty days after such producer or distributor shall have registered the name, current address and telephone number of the supervising rabbi or certifying organization who certifies the product as kosher with the department.

3-b. Any food commodity in package form which is marked as being certified by an organization, identified on the package by any symbol or is marked as being Kosher shall not be offered for sale by the producer or distributor of such food commodity until thirty days after such producer or distributor shall have registered the name, current address and telephone numbers of the certifying organization or the supervising rabbi with the department.

4. For the purposes of this section the term "food commodity in package form" shall be construed to mean a food commodity put up or packaged in any manner in advance of sale in units suitable for retail sale and which is not intended for consumption at point of manufacture.

5. All advertisements for food or food products sold as kosher under Rabbinical supervision must identify the name of rabbi or organization, if any, certifying such food or food product as being kosher.

6. Where a producer or distributor is required to register the identity of a supervising rabbi or certifying organization pursuant to the provisions of this section, such producer or distributor and the registered supervising rabbi or certifying organization shall immediately notify the department of any change in the identity of such registered supervising rabbi or certifying organization.

201-f. Kosher meat or poultry.

1. All meat or poultry which is sold, offered or exposed for sale and is represented as having been prepared in accordance with orthodox Hebrew religious requirements and which has not been soaked and salted immediately after slaughter on the premises where slaughtered:

   (a) shall have affixed to it a tag or plumba stating the date and time of day (a.m. or p.m.) of slaughter, and

(b) shall be washed in accordance with orthodox Hebrew religious requirements within seventy-two hours after slaughter, and within each subsequent seventy-two hour period, by a duly ordained orthodox rabbi or by a person authorized by him. The date and time of day (a.m. or p.m.) of each washing and the name of the person performing such duty shall be legibly indicated on the tag or plumba attached to the said meat or poultry.

2. No person shall sell, offer or expose for sale any meat or poultry which is represented as having been prepared in accordance with orthodox Hebrew religious requirements, unless such meat or poultry is in compliance with subdivision one of this section.

3. For purposes of this section:

(a) "Meat" means all primal and sub-primal parts of steers, cows, bulls, heifers, veal, lamb, and mutton, as defined by the commissioner in regulations.

(b) Liver shall be exempted from the requirements of paragraph (b) of subdivision one of this section.

4. The commissioner shall promulgate rules and regulations as are necessary to implement the provisions of this section, including but not limited to, the type of kosher identification to be affixed to each of the parts of such meat and poultry.

201-g. Listing of persons certifying as kosher.

No person, firm, association or corporation shall within this state manufacture, compound, brew, distill, produce, process, pack, sell, offer or expose for sale any non-prepackaged meat or meat preparations which is represented as or branded as kosher unless such person, firm, association or corporation has, in accordance with regulations set by the commissioner, filed with the department the name and address of the supervising person or organization certifying such product as kosher and the name and address of each person under whose supervision such product has been prepared, slaughtered, represented, branded or certified as kosher.

201-h. Parve or pareve.

It shall be unlawful to label food or food products with the words parve or pareve or in any way to indicate that the food or food product may be used or consumed indiscriminately with meat, poultry or dairy products according to Orthodox Hebrew requirements when such food or food products are impermissible for such use or consumption.

RULES AND REGULATIONS

Kosher Identifications on Meat and Food Products
(Except from Title 1 of Official Compilation of Codes,
Rules and Regulations of the State of New York)

PART 255
KOSHER IDENTIFICATIONS ON MEAT AND FOOD PRODUCTS

Section
255.1 Definitions.
255.2 Identification of kosher meat and meat products.
255.3 Kosher and kosher for Passover identification on containers.

Section 255.1 Definitions.

As used in this Part, the following terms shall mean:

(a) Plumba. The seal commonly used in the kosher industry, capable of being securely affixed, with the following indicia clearly and permanently displayed thereon:
    (1) the word "kosher" either in English or in Hebraic characters;
    (2) certain letters, figures, or emblems which will positively identify

such plumba with the particular slaughterhouse where the animal was slaughtered or processed.

(b) Tag. A tag, of whatever form, bearing the following information: (1) name and address of the slaughterhouse where the animal was slaughtered; (2) name of rabbi who sanctioned the kosher slaughtering of meat at the slaughterhouse named; and (3) date of slaughter.

(c) Kosher brand. Brand of a type approved by the United States Department of Agriculture.

(d) Washing. The use of unsalted, naturally cool water in such manner that the water reaches all parts of the interior and exterior surfaces of the meat.

255.2 Identification of kosher meat and meat products.

(a) All forequarters of steers, cows, bulls, heifers, and yearling calves sold or offered for sale by or in the possession of a kosher food dealer shall have securely affixed the following kosher identification to each of the following parts:

(1) Breast, rib, plate (outside), plate pieces (inside), chuck, shoulder, heart, lung, oxtail, tripe, milt (spleen), tender loin (hanger) -plumba and tag.

(2) Liver-two kosher brands and two plumbas, one of each to opposite ends of liver, so that if liver is cut in half through the vein each half will bear one plumba and one kosher brand.

(3) Feet-plumba and tag to each foot.

(4) Breads-plumba and tag to each pair.

(5) Brains-plumba to each brain, when sold separately from the head.

(6) Tongue-plumba and tag at the tip, and a kosher brand at the tip on smooth surface.

(7) Breastbone-incision made at the time of slaughter, in form of Hebrew characters, showing day of slaughter.

(8) Plate (inside) -two incisions made at the time of slaughter, in the form of Hebrew characters, showing day of slaughter.

(b) All foresaddles of veal sold or offered for sale by or in the possession of a kosher food dealer shall have securely affixed the following kosher identifications to each of the following parts:

(I) Breast-incision made at the time of slaughter, on each in the form of Hebrew characters, showing day of slaughter.

(2) Rack-two incisions made at the time of slaughter, on the inside, one of them on each side of the spine, in the form of Hebrew characters, showing the day of slaughter.

(3) Shoulder, but only when separated from the foresaddle at the time of slaughter-plumba and tag.

(4) Liver-plumba affixed to center of liver at the vein, and a kosher brand on the upper surface of liver.

(5) Haslett-plumba and tag through the heart and milt.

(6) Lung-plumba and tag.

(7) Feet-plumba and tag to each foot.

(8) Breads-one tag, and one plumba drawn through three pairs.

(9) Brains-plumba to each brain, when sold separately from the head.

(10) Tongue-plumba and tag at the tip, and a kosher brand at the tip on the smooth surface.

(c) All foresaddles of lamb and mutton sold or offered for sale by or in the possession of a kosher food dealer shall have securely affixed the following kosher identification of the following parts:

(l) Breast-incision made at the time of slaughter, on each in the form of Hebrew characters showing day of slaughter.

(2) Rack-two plumbas and two tags, one of each to either side of spine.

(3) Shoulder, but only if separated from foresaddle at time of slaughter-plumba and tag.

(4) Haslett-plumba and tag through the liver and milt.

(5) Tongue-one tag, and one plumba drawn through each group of six.

(6) Brains-plumba to each brain, when sold separately from the head.

(7) Liver-plumba and tag at center of liver, when sold separately from the haslett.

(d) Whenever any portion of meat from the animals referred to in subdivisions (a), (b) and (c) of this section is sold by a slaughterer as "kosher," a plumba and tag shall be securely attached to it at the time of slaughter.

(e) Washing of meats.

(1) All meats, except liver, shall be washed within 72 hours after slaughter, and within each subsequent 72-hour period, by a duly ordained Orthodox rabbi or by a person certified by him. The date and

time of the day (a.m. or p.m.) of each washing and the name of the person performing such duty shall be legibly indicated on all tags attached to the said meat.

(2) Meats to be washed enroute shall be governed by the following additional rules:

(i) The meat must be packed in such a manner as to allow said duly ordained Orthodox rabbi or his representative access to all the meats being washed as prescribed above.

(ii) The date and time of day of the washing shall be indicated on all tags or by means of a written statement securely attached inside the vehicle, signed by the rabbi supervising the washing, containing the date, place and time (a.m. or p.m.) of washing.

(iii) Upon receipt of the meat so washed enroute, the information contained in the written statement shall be legibly transferred on all the tags attached to the meat by the rabbi or his representative receiving said meat.

(3) When tongues, offal and other parts of meat that are packed in containers and are not deveined, soaked, salted and rinsed in accordance with the Jewish laws of koshering meat prior to shipping, they must be packed in containers that are sufficiently perforated to permit the free flow of water to reach all sides of said tongues, offal and other parts of meat packed therein and to enable the water to freely flow out again.

(4) When calves are shipped unflayed and part of the skin is detached from the meat, the water shall also reach every portion of the meat under the detached skin.

(5) All marks of kosher identification shall be removed by the owner or consignee from meat which has not been properly washed immediately after the time for washing has expired; provided, however, that liver shall be excepted from the requirements of this paragraph. All marks of kosher identification shall be removed by the owner or consignee from meat on which the date and time of day (a.m. or p.m.) of each washing have not been properly indicated on all tags attached thereto. Stamps, inscriptions and incisions of kosher marks of identification impressed on the meat shall be removed by the owner or consignee by blotting out and/or obliterating such marks of identification.

255.3. Kosher and kosher for Passover identification on containers.

All articles of food or food products, both liquid and solid, sold as kosher or kosher for Passover, in any container, as such word container is defined in section 192 of the Agriculture and Markets Law, bearing in any language a kosher or kosher for Passover identification by means of a brand, sticker, stamp, label, disc, cap, design or legend which might lead a reasonable person to believe that such articles of food or food products are kosher or kosher for Passover, shall have such kosher or kosher for Passover identification securely affixed on the outside of such container only by the manufacturer or packer at his premises. No person, other than such manufacturer or packer, shall possess or affix such marks of identification.

SHECHITA

One question often asked by people who are considering observing the laws of kashrus is, "Why does kosher meat have to cost so much?" We will attempt to answer this valid question by looking at the process of "shechita," Jewish ritual slaughter.

Ritual slaughter of animals differs in many ways from common techniques of slaughter. In ritual slaughter, we find caution and detail in every act. In this rabbinically supervised slaughter, the animal is killed with a knife. In this act we emphasize Jewish respect for the dignity of life. Great care is taken to use a knife that has been properly sharpened. The blade must be flawless, without a nick, and perfectly smooth, thus assuring that the kill will be quick, clean and painless to the animal.

This entire process begins with the *shochet* (ritual slaughterer) inspecting the knife for possible flaws and nicks. He does this by running the edge of his fingernail and finger up and down the blade. The slightest nick means that the knife must be resharpened. After this, he recites a short *Bracha* before beginning the actual *Shechita*.

This knife *(chalaf)* is usually about 6 inches long for chickens and 18 inches long for larger animals. The knife has no point at the end of it, and is of equal width from top to bottom. These precautions are necessary in order to guarantee that the neck of the animal will not be torn. The shochet must cut through the trachea and esophagus to the jugular vein very quickly and in a clean fashion. He must not kill the animal by stabbing it.

The animal's neck is first washed thoroughly to remove any sand particles in the fur which could cause a nick in the knife during slaughter. The shochet's hand must be very steady, and he must employ one continuous movement, carefully avoiding the spine. This cut only takes a few seconds and is a much more humane method of killing an animal than are such common practices as smashing the head, shooting the animal or scalding it while it is still alive.

Following the slaughter, the carcass is hung upside down so that the blood can drain properly. Then the shochet checks for adhesions on the lungs, which would indicate an abscess. If one is found, the animal is rejected as unkosher. Only about 30 percent of slaughtered animals can be used for kosher distribution.

At this point the *traibering* process is begun. The major blood vessels, nerves and forbidden fats will be removed.

The carcass is then divided into primal cuts. The next step is soaking the meat in water for 30 minutes. It is then salted for 1 hour, and then washed another 3 times.

A large slaughterhouse, when operating full time, may be able to slaughter 60 to 150 animals per hour. This process requires *shochtim* and rabbis on the premises for additional help in supervision. After the soaking and salting, a *plumba* (kosher seal) is either attached or stamped onto the meat or chicken.

Thus, the number of people needed to work in a kosher slaughtering and packing house is many times greater than in a non-kosher establishment and this considerably increases the price per pound of kosher meat. In addition, most butcher shops are relatively small businesses and must operate at a higher mark-up than do large chain supermarkets.

LAWS OF SHECHITA

There are 5 ways in which the slaughter becomes not kosher:

1) *Shehiya*. There must not be the least pause during the process of shechita.

2) *Derassa*. The process of slaughtering must be done by moving the knife back and forth — not through downward pressure. The knife, therefore, must be long enough to allow slaughtering without too much pressure. Moreover, the animal must be in such a position that undo pressure will not be placed on the knife.

3) *Chalada*. The shechita knife must be uncovered during the entire process of shechita. For this reason, the knife for shechita has a long and broad blade without a thin sharp end at the front or back.

4) *Hagrama*. The cut must be performed on the throat, between the level of the larynx and the lower part of the trachea and esophagus.

5) *Ikkur*. The trachea and esophagus must be cut through and not ripped out. The knife, therefore, must be very sharp and very smooth. The smallest nick in the blade will cause tearing. For this reason, the knife is checked for smoothness and sharpness before and after each shechita.

TREIFOS

There are eight types of mortal injury that render an animal unfit to be eaten. They are:

1. דרוסה Poisonous substance introduced into the body by an animal of prey hacking with its claws.
2. נקובה Organ walls perforated.
3. חסרה Complete organs or parts of them lacking.
4. נטולה Organs or parts of them having been removed.
5. קרועה Walls or covers of organs torn.

6. נפולה Shattered by a fall.

7. פסדנה Pipes split.

8. שבורה Fracture in bones.

TRAIBERING (NIKKUR – DEVEINING)

Before kashering meat, we must remove the blood vessels, nerves and fats that are forbidden to eat. This includes the sciatic nerve גיד הנשה. (בראשית כ״ג) Generally, *traibering* is done on the forequarter because there are so many areas in the hindquarter that would have to be removed that it is not economically feasible. In Israel, however, many people specialize in *traibering (Nikkur)* the hindquarter. But in America the hindquarter is generally sold for exclusively non-kosher use.

I. *Chailev* fats from the bull, calves, lamb, and steer are forbidden, as are the main tributary veins and arteries going through the neck and shoulders. We also *traiber* some membranes. *Traibering* must be done before soaking and salting. We do not use parts of the animal that touch the *chailev*.

II. The following cuts are always from the commonly used part of the animal: Deckel Roast, Apple Roast, Pepper Steak , Top of the Rib, Minute Steak, T.V. Roast, London Broil, Shoulder Roast, Cross Piece, Chuck Roast, Delmonica Steak, Cube Meat, Neck Meat, Brisket Strip, Brisket and Kaleche.

Beef Cuts

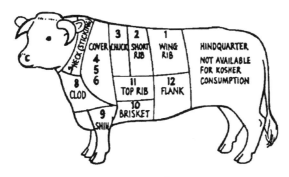

KASHERING MEAT

In order to kasher meat, it first must be soaked and salted. The first step in soaking is to wash off all of the blood. Soaking is done to enable the pores to open. The following are some important points in the process of soaking:

1. First the meat should be rinsed of all surface blood, then it can be soaked. The water should be at room temperature. In a vessel not normally used for cooking food, the meat should be soaked for half an hour. The water should then be shaken off so as not to dilute the salt. Then the meat should be salted and left to stand for one hour.

2. Kashering must be done within 72 hours of shechita, while the meat is fresh (not frozen). After that time, it can be koshered over an open fire. (Sprinkle a little salt on it before kashering on the fire.)

3. The salt used for kashering should be medium coarse.

4. After salting, one should rinse the meat 3 times.

KASHERING LIVER

1. First wash the liver, then place it on the fire (on a grill not normally used for broiling already kashered meats). Sprinkle it lightly with salt. Broil, then remove from the fire and wash it off.

2. Non-kashered meat or liver which were soaked for 24 hours are not kosher. An example of this would be a chicken defrosting in a refrigerator with liver inside.

3. If liver was cooked inside a chicken, it needs ביטול בששים (60 times more chicken than liver). Therefore, care should be taken to remove the liver that comes inside a whole chicken. Note: even chickens which are already kashered, the liver inside is NOT. In case of doubt, ask a competant Rabbi.

GLATT KOSHER

T he Torah states that "meat from an animal that has been torn in the field may not be eaten" (Exodus 22:30). This means that all animals intended for Jewish consumption, besides being of a kosher species and ritually slaughtered by a trained *shochet* (slaughterer), must be wholesome. Any lesion, rip, broken bone, illness, puncture or defect sufficient to kill the animal usually renders it *traif* (non-kosher). Although some defects may be visible while the animal is still alive, others require careful checking of the animal's internal organs to be sure it is free of any defects and diseases which could cause it to be non-kosher. It is particularly common to find adhesions to an animal's lung which indicate a puncture in the lung wall that would render the animal *traif*.

Until about 500 years ago, only meat from animals free of adhesions ("glatt") was used. Later, however, there were *halachic* (legal) authorities who permitted eating meat of animals with small adhesions on particular sections of the lung in case of dire need. If the adhesions are small, easily removable, and the lungs prove to be airtight (by inflation under water), the animal may be declared kosher, but not glatt.

Adhesions are not common in chickens in the U.S.A. and Canada. Therefore, *all* chicken meat here is considered glatt kosher.

Nowadays, one cannot even be sure that the "glatt kosher" meat one buys is truly "glatt." Since only a small percentage of animals are truly "glatt" (sometimes only one in 20), there is a shortage of true glatt kosher meat. Therefore, most suppliers have "watered down" the term "glatt" to include those animals which only have a few small adhesions, and some have diluted the term even more. Accordingly, it is possible that non-glatt meat of a *shochet* who is scrupulously precise with the glatt terminology may have fewer adhesions (i.e. be more glatt) than the boldly advertised "glatt kosher" meat of another. Even if the glatt label is accurate, that alone does not guarantee the meat to be of the highest kosher standards, since glatt does not, for example, refer to the quality of the shechita itself. Meat should only be bought from a source certified as kosher by a reliable rabbinic authority, whether the meat is glatt or not. When there is any doubt concerning the reliability of any particular kosher establishment, a reliable rabbinic authority should be consulted.

ILLUSTRATIONS OF KOSHER ANIMALS

Kosher animals with split hoofs and chew their cud:

Addax

Antelope

Bison

Cow

Deer

Gazelle

Goat

Ibex

Sheep

THE KOSHER BUTCHER SHOP

nce an animal has been correctly slaughtered and the meat has been certified as kosher, the person principally responsible for its kashrus is the butcher. Consequently, it is necessary to select a butcher who is himself G-d fearing and Torah observant. These are the qualities that the rabbis who certify the kashrus of butcher shops look for. They also examine the butcher's knowledge of the laws of keeping kosher, especially those laws that pertain to fresh meat. The butcher must also possess the knowledge and skills required to remove from meat the forbidden parts, fat and blood vessels (*"traibering"*.) Butchers must also know the laws of soaking and salting meat (kashering it), and the laws for storing meat not yet soaked-and-salted. If a butcher has no supervision and is accountable to no one, how can one be sure that the butcher either knows the laws or follows them—or, for that matter, that he only purchases kosher-certified meat?

Butchers who refuse to allow rabbinical supervision are open to suspicion of fraud, since great profit can be made from selling non-kosher meat as kosher. Some "self-supervised" kosher butchers boldly proclaim that their meat is cheaper. Certainly it is cheaper if the butcher does not take the costly man-hours necessary to *traiber* meat or to soak and salt it, and if he does not have to pay for rabbinical supervision. If your butcher is this type, you are possibly being misled into regular violation of Torah law—and you are also paying exorbitantly for the butcher's deceipt!

A butcher who declines supervision may think that he knows what he is doing, but he actually may not. He may have previously worked with an expert and now be under the impression that he knows all about kosher butchering but a certifying rabbi would be needed to ascertain whether the butcher knows how to traiber all cuts of meat, not just the few cuts he may have practiced under a fully-trained butcher's supervision. The rabbi would check that the butcher knows what equipment and utensils to use and how to keep from rendering the meat unkosher in the process of kashering (something that is rather easy to do). The butcher would need to demonstrate that he knows meat cannot be stored for longer than 3 days without being kashered, or at least washed down.

Meat and poultry require soaking in water and thorough salting before they are kosher for eating. But meat cannot be soaked and salted until after the forbidden fats, and blood vessels are removed. If the meat is soaked and salted before it is *traibered,* it is questionable. Special incisions must be made in the neck of poultry prior to soaking and salting to aid in the removal of blood. If the butcher waits more than 3 days before kashering the meat, the meat can only be kashered by broiling in the same manner as liver. Ground beef must be kashered before grinding. Storing any meat or poultry that has not been kashered in a bag or container which does not allow for free drainage of blood, renders the meat permanently non-kosher, if they haven't been kashered yet.

The rabbi must also test the butcher to see if he knows how to store and treat liver and other organ meats properly. It is necessary for the butcher to prove that he is aware that the kosher stamp on the carcass means the meat is kosher but does not preclude further treatment. This assumption is made by too many butchers and consumers.

How can the kosher consumer know how conscientious a butcher is unless a reliable rabbi has certified the butcher as competent and trustworthy? After all, many consumers are not aware that many butchers do not kasher meat as a matter of course. In fact, even butchers who kasher at a customer's request frequently do not kasher steaks and lamb chops because they assume that the consumer will broil them anyway, and will kasher them in the proper broiling process. The butcher, however, has both the legal and moral obligation to inform his customers. Rabbinic supervision provides the basis for a consumer's confidence in a butcher.

The trustworthiness of some butchers is suspect because of their practice of selling certain brands of chickens processed in warm water. Most authorities feel this cooks the blood so that it cannot be extracted by soaking and salting. Some plants where chickens are processed are "one-man operations." The same person slaughters the chickens, supervises his own slaughtering work, inspects the chickens after slaughter, and oversees the processing of the chickens. In reliably certified plants, these jobs are performed by at least four people. Finally, unlike the widely accepted brands of kosher poultry, the chickens from non-recommended plants are not always kashered prior to distribution. Since the chickens are not marked with the date of slaughter, the consumer has no way of knowing if the chickens can still be kashered.

In recent years, there have been several major scandals concerning chicken marketed nationally. In most instances, non-kosher chickens were substituted and fraudulently sold as kosher.

Certification by appropriate rabbinic authorities keeps such chickens from being foisted upon an unwary public. Rabbinic supervision ensures the consumer that the butcher, who is ultimately responsible for the kashrus of meat, is fully qualified and under supervision, which keeps him from purposely or inadvertently defrauding his customers.

HALACHIC SOURCES OF KASHRUS

NOT TO EAT THE SCIATIC NERVE

BERAISHIS XXXII

Therefore Bnei Yisrael must not eat the Gid Hanashe which is on the upper joint of the thigh, to this day, because he touched the Gid Hanashe at the upper joint of Yaakov's thigh.

בראשית ל'ב

לב עַל־כֵּן לֹא־יֹאכְלוּ בְנֵי־יִשְׂרָאֵל אֶת־גִּיד הַנָּשֶׁה אֲשֶׁר עַל־כַּף הַיָּרֵךְ עַד הַיּוֹם הַזֶּה כִּי נָגַע בְּכַף־יֶרֶךְ יַעֲקֹב בְּגִיד הַנָּשֶׁה׃

CHOMETZ ON PESACH

SHEMOS XIII

God spoke to Moshe as follows: 2. "Sanctify to Me every first-born, whatever opens the womb among the Bnei Yisrael, both of man and of beast is to me." 3. And Moshe said to the people: "Remember this day on which you went out from Mitzrayim, out from the house of bondage, that by a strong hand did *Hashem* bring you out from here, and for this reason no leaven shall be eaten. 4. Today you are going out, in the month of the growing grain! 5. and it shall be when *Hashem* will bring you to the land of the Canaanite and of the Hittite, of the Emorite, the Hivvite and the Yevusite, which he swore to your fathers to give to you, a land flowing with milk and honey, then you shall observe this ritual in this month. 6. Seven days you shall eat unleavened bread, and then, on the seventh day, you will make a festival to *Hashem*.

שמות י'ג

יג א וַיְדַבֵּר יְהֹוָה אֶל־מֹשֶׁה לֵּאמֹר׃ ב קַדֶּשׁ־לִי כָל־בְּכוֹר פֶּטֶר כָּל־רֶחֶם בִּבְנֵי יִשְׂרָאֵל בָּאָדָם וּבַבְּהֵמָה לִי הוּא׃ ג וַיֹּאמֶר מֹשֶׁה אֶל־הָעָם זָכוֹר אֶת־הַיּוֹם הַזֶּה אֲשֶׁר יְצָאתֶם מִמִּצְרַיִם מִבֵּית עֲבָדִים כִּי בְּחֹזֶק יָד הוֹצִיא יְהֹוָה אֶתְכֶם מִזֶּה וְלֹא יֵאָכֵל חָמֵץ׃ ד הַיּוֹם אַתֶּם יֹצְאִים בְּחֹדֶשׁ הָאָבִיב׃ ה וְהָיָה כִי־יְבִיאֲךָ יְהֹוָה אֶל־אֶרֶץ הַכְּנַעֲנִי וְהַחִתִּי וְהָאֱמֹרִי וְהַחִוִּי וְהַיְבוּסִי אֲשֶׁר נִשְׁבַּע לַאֲבֹתֶיךָ לָתֶת לָךְ אֶרֶץ זָבַת חָלָב וּדְבָשׁ וְעָבַדְתָּ אֶת־הָעֲבֹדָה הַזֹּאת בַּחֹדֶשׁ הַזֶּה׃ ו שִׁבְעַת יָמִים תֹּאכַל מַצֹּת וּבַיּוֹם הַשְּׁבִיעִי חַג לַיהֹוָה׃ ז

NON-KOSHER MEAT
FLESH FROM A LIVE ANIMAL

SHEMOS XXII

30. Men of a holy calling, you will be to me. You shall not eat meat that was torn off by beasts in the field, instead throw it to the dog(s).

שמות כ'ב

ל וְאַנְשֵׁי־קֹדֶשׁ תִּהְיוּן לִי וּבָשָׂר בַּשָּׂדֶה טְרֵפָה לֹא תֹאכֵלוּ לַכֶּלֶב תַּשְׁלִכוּן אֹתוֹ׃

74

SABBATICAL YEAR

שמות כ"ב

SHEMOS XXII MISHPATIM
10. And six years you shall sow your land and gather in its produce, 11. but in the seventh year you shall let it go and abandon it so that the poor among you may be able to eat from it, and whatever they leave over can be eaten by the beast(s) of the field; you shall do likewise with your vineyard and your olive tree.

י וְשֵׁשׁ שָׁנִים

תִּזְרַע אֶת־אַרְצֶךָ וְאָסַפְתָּ אֶת־תְּבוּאָתָהּ:
יא וְהַשְּׁבִיעִת תִּשְׁמְטֶנָּה וּנְטַשְׁתָּהּ וְאָכְלוּ אֶבְיֹנֵי
עַמֶּךָ וְיִתְרָם תֹּאכַל חַיַּת הַשָּׂדֶה כֵּן־תַּעֲשֶׂה
לְכַרְמְךָ לְזֵיתֶךָ׃

MEAT AND MILK

שמות ל"ד

SHEMOS XXXIV KI TISSA
18. The Festival of Matzos you shall keep; seven days you shall eat unleavened bread which I have commanded you, at the appointed meeting time of the month of the grain growing; for in the month of the growing grain did you go out from Mitzrayim.

יח אֶת־חַג הַמַּצּוֹת תִּשְׁמֹר שִׁבְעַת
יָמִים תֹּאכַל מַצּוֹת אֲשֶׁר צִוִּיתִךָ לְמוֹעֵד חֹדֶשׁ
הָאָבִיב כִּי בְּחֹדֶשׁ הָאָבִיב יָצָאתָ מִמִּצְרָיִם׃

26. ". ...You shall bring home into the House of Hashem, your God, the first of the first fruits of your soil; you shall not cook a young animal in the milk of its mother."

כו רֵאשִׁית בִּכּוּרֵי אַדְמָתְךָ תָּבִיא בֵּית יְהֹוָה
אֱלֹהֶיךָ לֹא־תְבַשֵּׁל גְּדִי בַּחֲלֵב אִמּוֹ: פ שביעי

BLOOD

ויקרא ג'

VAYIKRA III VAYIKRA
17. It shall be an evearlasting chok for your descendants in all your dwelling places: You shall not eat any fat, nor any blood.

יז חֻקַּת עוֹלָם לְדֹרֹתֵיכֶם בְּכֹל
מוֹשְׁבֹתֵיכֶם כָּל־חֵלֶב וְכָל־דָּם לֹא תֹאכֵלוּ: פ

BLOOD, FORBIDDEN FATS

ויקרא ז

VAYIKRA VII TZAV
22. Hashem spoke to Moshe (saying): 23. Speak to the sons of Yisrael (saying): You shall not eat any fat of oxen, sheep or goats. 24. and the fat of an animal that has died of itself and the fat of that which is a treifa may be used for any other purpose, but not for eating. 25. for whoever eats the fat of an animal of which a fire offering can be brought to Hashem, that person who eats it shall be uprooted from among his people. 26. and you shall eat no kind of blood in all your dwelling places, whether it be of bird or of lifestock. 27. any person who eats any kind of blood, that person shall be uprooted from among his people.

כב וַיְדַבֵּר יְהֹוָה אֶל־מֹשֶׁה לֵּאמֹר:
כג דַּבֵּר אֶל־בְּנֵי יִשְׂרָאֵל לֵאמֹר כָּל־חֵלֶב שׁוֹר
וְכֶשֶׂב וָעֵז לֹא תֹאכֵלוּ: כד וְחֵלֶב נְבֵלָה וְחֵלֶב
טְרֵפָה יֵעָשֶׂה לְכָל־מְלָאכָה וְאָכֹל לֹא תֹאכְלֻהוּ:
כה כִּי כָּל־אֹכֵל חֵלֶב מִן־הַבְּהֵמָה אֲשֶׁר יַקְרִיב
מִמֶּנָּה אִשֶּׁה לַיהֹוָה וְנִכְרְתָה הַנֶּפֶשׁ הָאֹכֶלֶת
מֵעַמֶּיהָ: כו וְכָל־דָּם לֹא תֹאכְלוּ בְּכֹל
מוֹשְׁבֹתֵיכֶם לָעוֹף וְלַבְּהֵמָה: כז כָּל־נֶפֶשׁ אֲשֶׁר
תֹּאכַל כָּל־דָּם וְנִכְרְתָה הַנֶּפֶשׁ הַהִוא מֵעַמֶּיהָ: פ

FORBIDDEN SPECIES IN THE WATER, EATING UNCLEAN ANIMALS, FORBIDDEN FISH, FORBIDDEN FOWL, RODENTS, CREEPING THINGS ON THE EARTH, WORMS, HUMAN FLESH, EATING MAASER SHENEI OUTSIDE OF YESUSHALAYIM

XI 1. *God* spoke to Moshe and to Aharon, and said to them: 2. Speak to the Bnei Yisrael saying: This is what you may eat of all the animals that live upon the land: 3. Whatever has a hoof and cleaves it completely into two hooves and at the same time chews it's cud among the animals, this you may eat. 4. But this you may not eat from among those that chew the cud and that are thus hoofed: The camel, because it chews the cud but does not form the proper hoof; it is unclean to you. 5. And the rabbit, because it chews the cud but does not have a hoof; it is unclean to you. 6. And the hare, because it chews the cud but does not have a hoof; it is unclean to you. 7. And the pig, because it has a hoof and cleaves the hoof completely but does not chew it's cud; it is unclean to you. 8. You shall not eat of their flesh and not touch their carcasses; they are unclean to you. 9. This you may eat of all that lives in the water; anything that has fins and scales in the water, in seas and in rivers, these you may eat. 10. But whatever does not have fins and scales in seas and in rivers, of all small creatures of the water and of all animals that live in the water; they are an abomination to you. 11. And they shall be an abomination to you, you shall not eat of their flesh, and their bodies removed from their habitat you shall hold in abomination. 12. Whatever has neither fins nor scales in the water, that is an abomination to you. 13. And these you shall hold in abomination from among the fowl; they shall not be eaten; they are an abomination; the *nesher*, the *peres* and the *azniyah;* 14. The *da'ah* and the *ayah* according to its species; 15. the *orev* according to its species; 16. the *bas hayaanah*, the *tahmas*, the *shahaf* and the *netz* according to its species; 17. the *kos*, the *shalakh* and the *yanshuf;* 18. The *tinshemes*, the *kaas* and the *raham;* 19. the *hasidah*, the *anafah* according to its species, the *duchifas* and the *atelef.* 20. Any winged creeping thing that goes upon four legs is an abomination to you. 21. Only this may you eat of all the winged creeping

ויקרא י״א

יא א וַיְדַבֵּר יְהֹוָה אֶל־
מֹשֶׁה וְאֶל־אַהֲרֹן לֵאמֹר אֲלֵהֶם: ב דַּבְּרוּ אֶל־בְּנֵי
יִשְׂרָאֵל לֵאמֹר זֹאת הַחַיָּה אֲשֶׁר תֹּאכְלוּ מִכָּל־
הַבְּהֵמָה אֲשֶׁר עַל־הָאָרֶץ: ג כֹּל ׀ מַפְרֶסֶת
פַּרְסָה וְשֹׁסַעַת שֶׁסַע פְּרָסֹת מַעֲלַת גֵּרָה בַּבְּהֵמָה
אֹתָהּ תֹּאכֵלוּ: ד אַךְ אֶת־זֶה לֹא תֹאכְלוּ מִמַּעֲלֵי
הַגֵּרָה וּמִמַּפְרִיסֵי הַפַּרְסָה אֶת־הַגָּמָל כִּי־מַעֲלֵה
גֵרָה הוּא וּפַרְסָה אֵינֶנּוּ מַפְרִיס טָמֵא הוּא לָכֶם:
ה וְאֶת־הַשָּׁפָן כִּי־מַעֲלֵה גֵרָה הוּא וּפַרְסָה לֹא
יַפְרִיס טָמֵא הוּא לָכֶם: ו וְאֶת־הָאַרְנֶבֶת כִּי־
מַעֲלַת גֵּרָה הִוא וּפַרְסָה לֹא הִפְרִיסָה טְמֵאָה
הִוא לָכֶם: ז וְאֶת־הַחֲזִיר כִּי־מַפְרִיס פַּרְסָה הוּא
וְשֹׁסַע שֶׁסַע פַּרְסָה וְהוּא גֵּרָה לֹא־יִגָּר טָמֵא
הוּא לָכֶם: ח מִבְּשָׂרָם לֹא תֹאכֵלוּ וּבְנִבְלָתָם לֹא
תִגָּעוּ טְמֵאִים הֵם לָכֶם: ט אֶת־זֶה תֹּאכְלוּ מִכֹּל
אֲשֶׁר בַּמָּיִם כֹּל אֲשֶׁר־לוֹ סְנַפִּיר וְקַשְׂקֶשֶׂת
בַּמַּיִם בַּיַּמִּים וּבַנְּחָלִים אֹתָם תֹּאכֵלוּ: י וְכֹל
אֲשֶׁר אֵין־לוֹ סְנַפִּיר וְקַשְׂקֶשֶׂת בַּיַּמִּים וּבַנְּחָלִים
מִכֹּל שֶׁרֶץ הַמַּיִם וּמִכֹּל נֶפֶשׁ הַחַיָּה אֲשֶׁר בַּמָּיִם
שֶׁקֶץ הֵם לָכֶם: יא וְשֶׁקֶץ יִהְיוּ לָכֶם מִבְּשָׂרָם לֹא
תֹאכֵלוּ וְאֶת־נִבְלָתָם תְּשַׁקֵּצוּ: יב כֹּל אֲשֶׁר אֵין־
לוֹ סְנַפִּיר וְקַשְׂקֶשֶׂת בַּמָּיִם שֶׁקֶץ הוּא לָכֶם:
יג וְאֶת־אֵלֶּה תְּשַׁקְּצוּ מִן־הָעוֹף לֹא יֵאָכְלוּ
שֶׁקֶץ הֵם אֶת־הַנֶּשֶׁר וְאֶת־הַפֶּרֶס וְאֵת הָעָזְנִיָּה:
יד וְאֶת־הַדָּאָה וְאֶת־הָאַיָּה לְמִינָהּ: טו אֵת כָּל־
עֹרֵב לְמִינוֹ: טז וְאֵת בַּת הַיַּעֲנָה וְאֶת־הַתַּחְמָס
וְאֶת־הַשָּׁחַף וְאֶת־הַנֵּץ לְמִינֵהוּ: יז וְאֶת־הַכּוֹס
וְאֶת־הַשָּׁלָךְ וְאֶת־הַיַּנְשׁוּף: יח וְאֶת־הַתִּנְשֶׁמֶת
וְאֶת־הַקָּאָת וְאֶת־הָרָחָם: יט וְאֵת הַחֲסִידָה
הָאֲנָפָה לְמִינָהּ וְאֶת־הַדּוּכִיפַת וְאֶת־הָעֲטַלֵּף:
כ כֹּל שֶׁרֶץ הָעוֹף הַהֹלֵךְ עַל־אַרְבַּע שֶׁקֶץ הוּא
לָכֶם: כא אַךְ אֶת־זֶה תֹּאכְלוּ מִכֹּל שֶׁרֶץ הָעוֹף

76

VAYIKRA XI SHEMINI

things that go upon four legs; those that have jointed legs above their feet, to hop with them upon the earth; 22. These of them you may eat: the *arbeh* according to its species; the *salam* according to its species, the *chargol* according to its species and the *chagav* according to its species. 23. Every winged creeping thing that has four legs is an abomination to you. 24. And concerning these you shall regard yourselves as unclean; whoever touches their carcass shall remain unclean until evening. 25. and whoever carries their carcass shall wash his garments and remain unclean until evening. 26. Concerning any animal that has hooves but does not cleave them and does not chew the cud; they are unclean to you; whatever touches them shall be unclean. 27. and also whatever goes on its paws among all animals that go upon four legs, they are unclean to you; whoever touches their carcass shall remain unclean until evening. 28. and whoever carries their carcass shall wash his garments and remain unclean until evening; they are unclean to you. 29. And this is what is unclean to you among the creeping things that creep upon the earth: the weasel, the mouse and the toad according to its species. 30. the hedgehog, the *koach*, the lizard, the *chomet* and the mole. 31. These are those that are unclean to you among all creeping things: whoever touches them when they are dead shall be unclean until evening. 39. and if any animal permitted for you to eat dies, he that touches its carcass shall be unclean until evening. 40. Whoever eats of its carcass must wash his garments and is unclean until evening; one who only carries its carcass must wash his garments and is unclean until evening. 41. and every creeping thing that creeps upon the earth, it is an abomination; it shall not be eaten. 42. Whatever goes upon the belly and whatever goes upon four legs, to whatever has many legs, of any creeping thing that creeps upon the earth, you shall not eat them because they are an abomination. 43. Do not make your souls an abomination with all the creeping things that creep, and do not make yourselves become tomeh. 44. For I, *Hashem*, am your God; therefore sanctify yourselves and then you will become holy, for I am holy, and do not make your souls unclean with all the creeping things that move upon the earth.

ויקרא י"א

הַהֹלֵךְ עַל־אַרְבַּע אֲשֶׁר־לָא (לו קרי) כְרָעַיִם מִמַּעַל לְרַגְלָיו לְנַתֵּר בָּהֵן עַל־הָאָרֶץ: כב אֶת־ אֵלֶּה מֵהֶם תֹּאכֵלוּ אֶת־הָאַרְבֶּה לְמִינֹו וְאֶת־ הַסָּלְעָם לְמִינֵהוּ וְאֶת־הֶחָרְגֹּל לְמִינֵהוּ וְאֶת־ הֶחָגָב לְמִינֵהוּ: כג וְכֹל שֶׁרֶץ הָעֹוף אֲשֶׁר־לֹו אַרְבַּע רַגְלָיִם שֶׁקֶץ הוּא לָכֶם: כד וּלְאֵלֶּה תִּטַּמָּאוּ כָּל־הַנֹּגֵעַ בְּנִבְלָתָם יִטְמָא עַד־הָעָרֶב: כה וְכָל־הַנֹּשֵׂא מִנִּבְלָתָם יְכַבֵּס בְּגָדָיו וְטָמֵא עַד־הָעָרֶב: כו לְכָל־הַבְּהֵמָה אֲשֶׁר הִוא מַפְרֶסֶת פַּרְסָה וְשֶׁסַע אֵינֶנָּה שֹׁסַעַת וְגֵרָה אֵינֶנָּה מַעֲלָה טְמֵאִים הֵם לָכֶם כָּל־הַנֹּגֵעַ בָּהֶם יִטְמָא: כז וְכֹל הֹולֵךְ עַל־כַּפָּיו בְּכָל־הַחַיָּה הַהֹלֶכֶת עַל־אַרְבַּע טְמֵאִים הֵם לָכֶם כָּל־הַנֹּגֵעַ בְּנִבְלָתָם יִטְמָא עַד־הָעָרֶב: כח וְהַנֹּשֵׂא אֶת־נִבְלָתָם יְכַבֵּס בְּגָדָיו וְטָמֵא עַד־הָעָרֶב טְמֵאִים הֵמָּה לָכֶם: ס כט וְזֶה לָכֶם הַטָּמֵא בַּשֶּׁרֶץ הַשֹּׁרֵץ עַל־הָאָרֶץ הַחֹלֶד וְהָעַכְבָּר וְהַצָּב לְמִינֵהוּ: ל וְהָאֲנָקָה וְהַכֹּחַ וְהַלְּטָאָה וְהַחֹמֶט וְהַתִּנְשָׁמֶת: לא אֵלֶּה הַטְּמֵאִים לָכֶם בְּכָל־הַשָּׁרֶץ כָּל־הַנֹּגֵעַ בָּהֶם בְּמֹתָם יִטְמָא עַד־הָעָרֶב: לב וְכֹל אֲשֶׁר־יִפֹּל הַמְּבֻלָּה אֲשֶׁר־הִיא לָכֶם לְאָכְלָה הַנֹּגֵעַ בְּנִבְלָתָהּ יִטְמָא עַד־הָעָרֶב: ס וְהָאֹכֵל מִנִּבְלָתָהּ יְכַבֵּס בְּגָדָיו וְטָמֵא עַד־הָעָרֶב וְהַנֹּשֵׂא אֶת־נִבְלָתָהּ יְכַבֵּס בְּגָדָיו וְטָמֵא עַד־הָעָרֶב: מא וְכָל־הַשֶּׁרֶץ הַשֹּׁרֵץ עַל־הָאָרֶץ שֶׁקֶץ הוּא לֹא יֵאָכֵל: מב כֹּל הֹולֵךְ עַל־גָּחֹון (ו"י רגחון חצי החתרה באותיות חורי רבח") וְכֹל הֹולֵךְ עַל־אַרְבַּע עַד כָּל־מַרְבֵּה רַגְלַיִם לְכָל־הַשֶּׁרֶץ הַשֹּׁרֵץ עַל־הָאָרֶץ לֹא תֹאכְלוּם כִּי־שֶׁקֶץ הֵם: מג אַל־תְּשַׁקְּצוּ אֶת־ נַפְשֹׁתֵיכֶם בְּכָל־הַשֶּׁרֶץ הַשֹּׁרֵץ וְלֹא תִטַּמְּאוּ בָּהֶם וְנִטְמֵתֶם בָּם: מד כִּי אֲנִי יְהוָה אֱלֹהֵיכֶם וְהִתְקַדִּשְׁתֶּם וִהְיִיתֶם קְדֹשִׁים כִּי קָדֹושׁ אָנִי וְלֹא תְטַמְּאוּ אֶת־נַפְשֹׁתֵיכֶם בְּכָל־הַשֶּׁרֶץ הָרֹמֵשׂ עַל־הָאָרֶץ:

FORBIDDEN MEATS

VAYIKRA XXII EMOR

8. He must not eat anything that has died of itself, and is a nevaila or that has been torn, to become unclean by it;

ויקרא כ״ב

ח וְנִבְלָה וּטְרֵפָה לֹא יֹאכַל לְטָמְאָה־בָהּ אֲנִי יְהֹוָה: ס

NEW WHEAT

VAYIKRA XXIII EMOR

9. *God* spoke to Moshe saying: 10. "Speak to the Bnei Yisrael and say to them: When you come to the land which I give you and you reap its harvest, you shall bring the *omer* of your first reaping to the priest, 11. and he shall wave the *omer* before *Hashem* willingly; on the day after that Sabbath shall the priest wave it. 12. And on the day when you wave the *omer* you shall offer an unblemished yearling sheep as an olah offering to *God.* 13. and its homage offering, two tenths of fine wheat flour mixed with oil, a fire offering to *God,* as an expression of compliance, and its wine libation one fourth of a *hin.* 14. and you shall not eat bread, parched flour and green ears until that day, until you have made the offering of your God; an everlasting statute for your descendants in all your dwelling places.

ויקרא כ״ג

ס וַיְדַבֵּר יְהֹוָה אֶל־מֹשֶׁה לֵּאמֹר: י דַּבֵּר אֶל־בְּנֵי יִשְׂרָאֵל וְאָמַרְתָּ אֲלֵהֶם כִּי־תָבֹאוּ אֶל־הָאָרֶץ אֲשֶׁר אֲנִי נֹתֵן לָכֶם וּקְצַרְתֶּם אֶת־קְצִירָהּ וַהֲבֵאתֶם אֶת־עֹמֶר רֵאשִׁית קְצִירְכֶם אֶל־הַכֹּהֵן: יא וְהֵנִיף אֶת־הָעֹמֶר לִפְנֵי יְהֹוָה לִרְצֹנְכֶם מִמָּחֳרַת הַשַּׁבָּת יְנִיפֶנּוּ הַכֹּהֵן: יב וַעֲשִׂיתֶם בְּיוֹם הֲנִיפְכֶם אֶת־הָעֹמֶר כֶּבֶשׂ תָּמִים בֶּן־שְׁנָתוֹ לְעֹלָה לַיהֹוָה: יג וּמִנְחָתוֹ שְׁנֵי עֶשְׂרֹנִים סֹלֶת בְּלוּלָה בַשֶּׁמֶן אִשֶּׁה לַיהֹוָה רֵיחַ נִיחֹחַ וְנִסְכֹּה (תסכו קרי) יַיִן רְבִיעִת הַהִין: יד וְלֶחֶם וְקָלִי וְכַרְמֶל לֹא תֹאכְלוּ עַד־עֶצֶם הַיּוֹם הַזֶּה עַד הֲבִיאֲכֶם אֶת־קָרְבַּן אֱלֹהֵיכֶם חֻקַּת עוֹלָם לְדֹרֹתֵיכֶם בְּכֹל מֹשְׁבֹתֵיכֶם: ס

SABBATICAL YEAR

VAYIKRA XXV BEHAR

XXV 1. *Hashem* spoke to Moshe on Mount Sinai saying: 2. Speak to the BneiYisrael and say to them: When you come into the land which I give you, the land shall observe a Sabbath to *Hashem.* 3. Six years you shall sow your field and six years you shall prune your vineyard and gather in its produce, 4. But in the seventh year there shall be a Sabbath observed by cessation from work for the land, a Sabbath to *God;* you shall not sow your field nor prune your vineyard. 5. You shall not harvest the aftergrowth of your harvest and not gather in the grapes from a vine left untended; there shall be a year of cessation from work for the land. 6. But the Sabbath produce of the land shall be permitted for you as food, for yourself and for your servant and for your handmaid, also for your hired worker and your tenant who live with you. 7. And for your cattle, as well as for your animals that are in your land shall all its produce be for food.

ויקרא כ״ה

כה א וַיְדַבֵּר יְהֹוָה אֶל־מֹשֶׁה בְּהַר סִינַי לֵאמֹר: ב דַּבֵּר אֶל־בְּנֵי יִשְׂרָאֵל וְאָמַרְתָּ אֲלֵהֶם כִּי תָבֹאוּ אֶל־הָאָרֶץ אֲשֶׁר אֲנִי נֹתֵן לָכֶם וְשָׁבְתָה הָאָרֶץ שַׁבָּת לַיהֹוָה: ג שֵׁשׁ שָׁנִים תִּזְרַע שָׂדֶךָ וְשֵׁשׁ שָׁנִים תִּזְמֹר כַּרְמֶךָ וְאָסַפְתָּ אֶת־תְּבוּאָתָהּ: ד וּבַשָּׁנָה הַשְּׁבִיעִת שַׁבַּת שַׁבָּתוֹן יִהְיֶה לָאָרֶץ שַׁבָּת לַיהֹוָה שָׂדְךָ לֹא תִזְרָע וְכַרְמְךָ לֹא תִזְמֹר: ה אֵת סְפִיחַ קְצִירְךָ לֹא תִקְצוֹר וְאֶת־עִנְּבֵי נְזִירֶךָ לֹא תִבְצֹר שְׁנַת שַׁבָּתוֹן יִהְיֶה לָאָרֶץ: ו וְהָיְתָה שַׁבַּת הָאָרֶץ לָכֶם לְאָכְלָה לְךָ וּלְעַבְדְּךָ וְלַאֲמָתֶךָ וְלִשְׂכִירְךָ וּלְתוֹשָׁבְךָ הַגָּרִים עִמָּךְ: ז וְלִבְהֶמְתְּךָ וְלַחַיָּה אֲשֶׁר בְּאַרְצֶךָ תִּהְיֶה כָל־תְּבוּאָתָהּ לֶאֱכֹל: ס

78

MITZVA OF TAKING CHALLA

במדבר ט"ז

BAMIDBAR XV SHELACH LECHHA

17. *Hashem* spoke to Moshe saying: 18. "Speak to the Bnei Yisrael and say to them: When you come into the land to which I am bringing you, 19. when you eat of the bread of the land, you shall lift from it an uplifted donation for *Hashem* 20. As the first portion from your kneading troughs you shall lift out a cake of bread as an uplifted donation. Like the uplifted donation from your threshing floor, so shall you lift up this one. 21. From the first portion from your kneading troughs shall you give to *God* a Teruma for your descendants.

ששי יז וַיְדַבֵּר יְהֹוָה אֶל־מֹשֶׁה לֵּאמֹר: יח דַּבֵּר אֶל־בְּנֵי יִשְׂרָאֵל וְאָמַרְתָּ אֲלֵהֶם בְּבֹאֲכֶם אֶל־הָאָרֶץ אֲשֶׁר אֲנִי מֵבִיא אֶתְכֶם שָׁמָּה: יט וְהָיָה בַּאֲכָלְכֶם מִלֶּחֶם הָאָרֶץ תָּרִימוּ תְרוּמָה לַיהֹוָה: כ רֵאשִׁית עֲרִסֹתֵכֶם חַלָּה תָּרִימוּ תְרוּמָה כִּתְרוּמַת גֹּרֶן כֵּן תָּרִימוּ אֹתָהּ: כא מֵרֵאשִׁית עֲרִסֹתֵיכֶם תִּתְּנוּ לַיהֹוָה תְּרוּמָה לְדֹרֹתֵיכֶם: ס

EATING A LIMB FROM A LIVE ANIMAL

דברים י"ב

DEVARIM XII RE-EH

20. When *Hashem* will extend your territory as He has promised you, and you will say: "I want to eat meat," because you crave to eat meat, then you may eat meat according to all the desire of your will. 21. Because the place that *God*, your God, will choose, to give His Name a habitation there, will be far away from you; you shall slaughter of your cattle and of your sheep that *God* has given you, in the manner that I have commanded you, and you shall eat within your gates, according to all the desires of your will. 22. However, as the deer and the doe is eaten, so shall you eat it; the unclean and the pure may eat it together. 23. Only remain firm not to eat blood; for the blood is the soul. Also, do not eat the soul with the flesh. 24 Do not eat it! Pour it out upon the ground like water. 25. Do not eat it! So that it may go well with you and with your children after you; for you will be doing that which is upright in the eyes of *God*.

ס כ כִּי־יַרְחִיב יְהֹוָה אֱלֹהֶיךָ אֶת־גְּבֻלְךָ כַּאֲשֶׁר דִּבֶּר־לָךְ וְאָמַרְתָּ אֹכְלָה בָשָׂר כִּי־תְאַוֶּה נַפְשְׁךָ לֶאֱכֹל בָּשָׂר בְּכָל־אַוַּת נַפְשְׁךָ תֹּאכַל בָּשָׂר: כא כִּי־יִרְחַק מִמְּךָ הַמָּקוֹם אֲשֶׁר יִבְחַר יְהֹוָה אֱלֹהֶיךָ לָשׂוּם שְׁמוֹ שָׁם וְזָבַחְתָּ מִבְּקָרְךָ וּמִצֹּאנְךָ אֲשֶׁר נָתַן יְהֹוָה לְךָ כַּאֲשֶׁר צִוִּיתִךָ וְאָכַלְתָּ בִּשְׁעָרֶיךָ בְּכֹל אַוַּת נַפְשֶׁךָ: כב אַךְ כַּאֲשֶׁר יֵאָכֵל אֶת־הַצְּבִי וְאֶת־הָאַיָּל כֵּן תֹּאכְלֶנּוּ הַטָּמֵא וְהַטָּהוֹר יַחְדָּו יֹאכְלֶנּוּ: כג רַק חֲזַק לְבִלְתִּי אֲכֹל הַדָּם כִּי הַדָּם הוּא הַנָּפֶשׁ וְלֹא־תֹאכַל הַנֶּפֶשׁ עִם־הַבָּשָׂר: כד לֹא תֹּאכְלֶנּוּ עַל־הָאָרֶץ תִּשְׁפְּכֶנּוּ כַּמָּיִם: כה לֹא תֹּאכְלֶנּוּ לְמַעַן יִיטַב לְךָ וּלְבָנֶיךָ אַחֲרֶיךָ כִּי־תַעֲשֶׂה הַיָּשָׁר בְּעֵינֵי יְהֹוָה:

FORBIDDEN MEAT, FORBIDDEN FOWL

דברים י"ד

DEVARIM XIV RE-EH

3. You shall not eat any abominable thing. 4. This is the livestock you may eat: ox, lamb and kid. 5. Doe, deer and *yahmur, akko, dishon, te'o* and *zemer.* 6. and every animal that forms a hoof and cleaves it completely into two hooves and at the same time chews the cud among the animals, this you may eat. 7. But this you may not eat from among those that

ג לֹא תֹאכַל כָּל־תּוֹעֵבָה: ד זֹאת הַבְּהֵמָה אֲשֶׁר תֹּאכֵלוּ שׁוֹר שֵׂה כְשָׂבִים וְשֵׂה עִזִּים: ה אַיָּל וּצְבִי וְיַחְמוּר וְאַקּוֹ וְדִישֹׁן וּתְאוֹ וָזָמֶר: ו וְכָל־בְּהֵמָה מַפְרֶסֶת פַּרְסָה וְשֹׁסַעַת שֶׁסַע שְׁתֵּי פְרָסוֹת מַעֲלַת גֵּרָה בַּבְּהֵמָה אֹתָהּ תֹּאכֵלוּ: ז אַךְ אֶת־זֶה לֹא תֹאכְלוּ מִמַּעֲלֵי הַגֵּרָה

79

chew the cud and that are thus clovenhoofed: the camel, the hare and the rabbit, because they chew the cud but have not formed a hoof; they are unclean to you. 8. and the pig, because it forms hooves but does not chew the cud; it is unclean to you; you shall not eat of their flesh nor touch their carcasses.

9. This you may eat of all that is in the water: whatever has fins and scales you may eat. 10. but whatever does not have fins and scales you may not eat; it is unclean to you. 11. You may eat any clean bird.to you. 11. You may eat any clean bird. 12. But of these you may not eat: the *nesher*, the peres and the *ozniyah;* 13. the *ra'ah*, the *ayah* and the *dayah*, according to their species; 14.any *orev* according to its species; 15. the *bas ha-yaanah*, the *tahmas*, the *shahaf* and the *netz*, according to its species; 16. the *kos*, the *yanshuf* and the *tinshomes* 17. the *ka'aas* and the *rahamah* and the *shalach;* 18. the *hasidah* and the *anafah*, according to its species; the *dukhiphas* and the *atalef*. 19. Every winged creeping thing is unclean to you; they may not be eaten. 20. Any clean flying creature you may eat. 21. You shall not eat any carrion; you may give it to one who has come in from outside, who is within your gates, that he may eat it, or sell it to a foreigner, for you are a holy people to *Hashem* , your God; you shall not cook a young animal in the milk of its mother.

וּמִמַּפְרִיסֵי הַפַּרְסָה הַשְּׁסוּעָה אֶת־הַגָּמָל וְאֶת־הָאַרְנֶבֶת וְאֶת־הַשָּׁפָן כִּי־מַעֲלֵה גֵרָה הֵמָּה וּפַרְסָה לֹא הִפְרִיסוּ טְמֵאִים הֵם לָכֶם: ח וְאֶת־הַחֲזִיר כִּי־מַפְרִיס פַּרְסָה הוּא וְלֹא גֵרָה טָמֵא הוּא לָכֶם מִבְּשָׂרָם לֹא תֹאכֵלוּ וּבְנִבְלָתָם לֹא תִגָּעוּ: ס ט אֶת־זֶה תֹּאכְלוּ מִכֹּל אֲשֶׁר בַּמָּיִם כֹּל אֲשֶׁר־לוֹ סְנַפִּיר וְקַשְׂקֶשֶׂת תֹּאכֵלוּ: י וְכֹל אֲשֶׁר אֵין־לוֹ סְנַפִּיר וְקַשְׂקֶשֶׂת לֹא תֹאכֵלוּ טָמֵא הוּא לָכֶם: ס יא כָּל־צִפּוֹר טְהֹרָה תֹּאכֵלוּ: יב וְזֶה אֲשֶׁר לֹא־תֹאכְלוּ מֵהֶם הַנֶּשֶׁר וְהַפֶּרֶס וְהָעָזְנִיָּה: יג וְהָרָאָה וְאֶת־הָאַיָּה וְהַדַּיָּה לְמִינָהּ: יד וְאֵת כָּל־עֹרֵב לְמִינוֹ: טו וְאֵת בַּת הַיַּעֲנָה וְאֶת־הַתַּחְמָס וְאֶת־הַשָּׁחַף וְאֶת־הַנֵּץ לְמִינֵהוּ: טז אֶת־הַכּוֹס וְאֶת־הַיַּנְשׁוּף וְהַתִּנְשָׁמֶת: יז וְהַקָּאָת וְאֶת־הָרָחָמָה וְאֶת־הַשָּׁלָךְ: יח וְהַחֲסִידָה וְהָאֲנָפָה לְמִינָהּ וְהַדּוּכִיפַת וְהָעֲטַלֵּף: יט וְכֹל שֶׁרֶץ הָעוֹף טָמֵא הוּא לָכֶם לֹא יֵאָכֵלוּ: כ כָּל־עוֹף טָהוֹר תֹּאכֵלוּ: מ לֹא תֹאכְלוּ כָל־נְבֵלָה לַגֵּר אֲשֶׁר־בִּשְׁעָרֶיךָ תִּתְּנֶנָּה וַאֲכָלָהּ אוֹ מָכֹר לְנָכְרִי כִּי עַם קָדוֹשׁ אַתָּה לַיהֹוָה אֱלֹהֶיךָ לֹא־תְבַשֵּׁל גְּדִי בַּחֲלֵב אִמּוֹ: ס

SOURCES OF FORBIDDEN FOODS
AND THEIR CATEGORIES

איסורי אכילה מדאורייתא

אזהרות לאו -עונש מלקות

א. אבר מן החי -ולא תאכל הנפש עם הבשר (דברים י"ב, כ"ג; חולין ק"ב ע"ב)

ב. בהמה וחיה טמאה - אך את זה לא תאכלו ממעלי הגרה (ויקרא י"א, ד)

ג. בשר וחלב - לא תבשל גדי בחלב אמו (שמות ל"ד, כ"ו; חולין קט"ו ע"ב)

ד. בשר מן החי - ובשר בשדה טרפה לא תאכלו (שמות כ"ב, ל; חולין ק"ב ע"ב)

ה. גיד הנשה - על כן לא יאכלו בני ישראל את גיד הנשה (בראשית ל"ב, ל"ג)

ו. דגים טמאים - וכל אשר אין לו סנפיר וקשקשת במים ובנחלים וגו' לא תאכלו
(ויקרא י"א י-י"א)

ז. טרפה - ובשר בשדה טרפה לא תאכלו (שמות כ"ב ט; חולין ס"ח ע"ב)

ח. נבלה - לא תאכלו כל נבלה (דברים י"ד, כ"א)

ט. עוף טמא - ואת אלה תשקצו מן העוף לא יאכלו שקץ הם (ויקרא י"א, י"ג)

י. שרץ העוף - וכל שרץ העוף טמא הוא לכם לא יאכלו (דברים י"ד, י"ט)

יא. שרץ הארץ - וכל השרץ השורץ על הארץ שקץ הוא לא יאכל (ויקרא י"א, מ"א)

יב. שרץ המים - אל תשקצו את נפשותיכם בכל השרץ (ויקרא י"א, מ"א)

יג. רמשים - ולא תטמאו את נפשותיכם בכל השרץ הרמש על הארץ (ויקרא י"א, מ"ד)

יד. תולעת פירות באויר - לכל השרץ השרץ על הארץ לא תאכלו (ויקרא י"א, מ"ב)

טו. איסורי אכילה בבכור

טז. איסורי אכילה מתקרובת אבודה זרה

איסורי כרת באכילה

א. דם - וכל דם לא תאכלו (ויקרא ג', י"ז)

ב. חלב - כל חלב שור וכשב ועז לא תאכלו (ויקרא ז, כ"ג)

ג. חמץ בפסח - ולא יאכל חמץ (שמות י"ג, ג')

מיתה בידי שמים על איסורי אכילה

א. טבל - ולא יחללו את קדשי בני ישראל את אשר ירימו לה' (ויקרא כ"ב, ט"ו)

ב. תרומה וביכורים לזר - ומתו בו כי יחללהו אני ה' מקדשם וכל זר לא יאכל קדש
(ויקרא כ"ב, י')

איסור עשה על אכילה

א. בשר אדם - זאת החיה אשר תאכלו (ויקרא י,א, ב')

ב. מעשר שני חוץ לירושלים לפני שנכנס לירושלים (ויקרא י"א, ב')

ג. פירות שביעית אחר זמן הביעור - ולבהמתך ולחיה אשר בארצך תהיה כל תבואתה
לאכל (ויקרא כ"ה, ז'; פסחים כ"ב ע"ב)

איסורי אכילה מדרבנן

א. בישול עכו"ם (עבודה זרה ל"ח ע"א) - שמא יאכילנו דבר טמא (רש"י) או משום חתנות
(תוספות)

ב. גבינת עכו"ם - שמעמידים אותה בעור של קיבת נבלה (עבודה זרה כ"ט ע"ב)

ג. חלב עכו"ם - שמא עירבו בו חלב מבהמה טמאה (עבודה זרה כ"ט ע"ב)

ד. סתם יין עכו"ם - משום חתנות (שבת י"ז ע"ב)

ה. פת עכו"ם - משום התנות (שבת י"ז ע"ב)

ו. איסור ללכת לסעודת עכו"ם - משום חתנות

Some General Laws of Kashrus

1. The prohibition of **meat and milk** relating to domestic animals is the following:

 a. They cannot be cooked together.

 b. If they were cooked together, they are forever forbidden to eat.

 c. One cannot even derive benefit from this forbidden mixture. (This is a common problem with dog and cat foods, which often contains cheese, whey, and beef.)

Although these laws extend to fowl as well, the איסור of deriving benefit does not apply here. An example of this is dog food, which contains chicken and whey, and is allowed to be used by the kosher consumer for his pets.

2. Once meat is eaten, one must wait a period of time before eating dairy foods. According to most authorities one must wait 6 hours before eating dairy. This is the common practice among most Jews. However, some communities have a tradition of allowing dairy to be eaten following meat after a wait of 1 to 3 hours. People should follow their family tradition. This opinion follows the ruling of *Tosfos*. This Halacha of separating meat and milk extends even to the point of not allowing two people to eat at the same table while one is eating dairy and the other is eating meat. (When necessary, however, some sort of divider can be placed between them.) This is true only when the people know each other. In the case of two strangers in a restaurant, for instance, this does not apply.

3. The only time that it is necessary to wait after eating dairy foods is in the case of **hard cheese.** Cheese is considered hard only after being aged for 6 months or longer. Currently in the U.S., almost all cheeses that are available to the kosher consumer are aged only 60 days.

4. Utensils: In order to observe the above laws carefully, we use separate utensils for dairy and meat products. This separation affects cooking utensils

as well as eating utensils. It is therefore necessary to keep one set of cookware and utensils for dairy use and another set for meat use. Unfortunately, at times, we find that the two sets of utensils get mixed up and confused. When this happens, it is necessary to consult a competent Rabbi.

Generally speaking, the following rules apply:

a. Cold utensils don't contaminate each other and when they have been used only in a cold state, they do not require kashering. The exception is if they become *kovush,* such as in the case where milk drops on a meat plate. If the milk remains there for 24 hours or more, the utensil becomes non-kosher.

b. Even <u>cold</u> utensils that were used for "cold" foods, if the food was of a sharp nature, such as onions, they follow the rules of "hot" foods. This is true only in the case of *Duchka Desokino,* where a knife was used to slice the food. This is due to the pressure caused by the slicing.

c. In a case where food that was cut by utensils of the opposite type (i.e., a dairy knife cutting hot meat,) the cutting utensil requires kashering. The food may not be kosher depending on its size.

d. Glassware is usually considered pareve and cannot take on the characteristic of either meat or dairy when they are used for drinking or eating but not for cooking. This is true of Arcolac and Corelle. <u>Note:</u> Pyrex <u>is not</u> included in above.

5. The **general** rules of kashering a utensil are as follows:

a. Only metal utensils can be kashered.

b. We only kosher utensils from dairy to meat or vice versa when they have become non-kosher, or when we are kashering them anyway for Pesach. It is not allowed to kasher from one status to the other (meat and dairy) year round for mere convenience.

c.   Plastic, synthetic rubber, melmac, porcelain, pyrex, Corningware, Teflon and Silverstone cannot be kashered.

d.   When an article can be kashered, the rule is that "as it absorbed, so it will expel". Therefore, items used with liquid can be kashered with liquid. However, items used directly "in the fire", without liquid, such as a cookie sheet, are harder to kasher. These would need to be heated directly with a very hot temperature such as a torch.

6. Dishwashers, according to Rav Moshe Feinstein, ZT"L, can be used for dairy and meat utensils. This is true even with the porcelain lined dishwashers. Care must be taken to clean the drain before switching. However, it is **necessary** to maintain separate racks for dairy and meat dishes. It is recommended, as well, to run the dishwasher with soap (empty) in between dairy and meat use. This leniency does **not apply** to using the year round dishwasher for Pesach.

7. Tablecloths and napkins can be used for dairy or meat **provided** they are cloth and not plastic. The tablecloth must be washed between uses.

8. A hot water urn can be used to place water in dairy or meat utensils. This is only true when the urn is not used for anything other than water or other pareve substances.

9. Sinks should be used separately for dairy and meat utensils. In case of a sink that is not kosher, or when only one sink is available, a plastic tub or insert should be used. Only sinks made of metal can be kashered.

10. A **blender** or **food processor** needs separate containers and blades for dairy and meat use.

11. The range (cooktop) can be used for dairy and for meat according to most opinions. The reason is that the metal prongs are always in contact with the

fire, making them kosher.

12. A refrigerator and freezer can be used for both dairy and meat products. Care should be taken not to allow anything to drip from the dairy to the meat products or vice versa.

When moving into a new home, where the dishwasher was not kosher, Rav Moshe Feinstein, ZT"L, is of the opinion that one should wait for 12 months before using the dishwasher. During this time, the dishwasher should not be used at all. After 12 months, the dishwasher should be run 3 cycles with detergent. At the completion of this procedure, the dishwasher and racks may be used.

13. There can be a problem when one has a non-Jewish maid in the house. Meat, as well as other kosher items (utensils etc.) cannot be left unattended where a mishap can occur. If the non-Jewish maid knows that a Jew will be coming into the house, periodically, unannounced and unscheduled, this would alleviate this problem. It is highly advisable for one who has a non-Jewish maid to have locks on utensil and food cabinets to avoid this problem. Another alternative is to arrange with a Jewish neighbor to come in at irregular intervals during the day.

14. A toaster oven cannot be used for both dairy and meat. It must be designated for dairy or meat only. Since some companies test the toaster first with non-kosher bread, check for breadcrumbs. If found, ask your Rav what to do.

15. Meat and fish may not be eaten together. Nevertheless, fish may be cooked in either a dairy or meat pot and eaten with the appropriate cutlery corresponding to the status of the pot in which the fish was cooked.

16. If a person is cooking soup with meat in it and tastes it to see if the flavoring is right, and then spits out the soup, without swallowing any, he is considered to be "meaty" (fleishig).

17. Meat vitamins, such as liver pills, do not make a person "meaty". It is

not necessary to wait 6 hours after swallowing these pills.

18. Although normally, it is not permissible for a person to kasher his silverware from milk to meat (or visa versa,) if he receive expensive silverware as a gift, he may kasher it.

CHOMETZ ON PESACH

"Chometz" is any substance containing leavening from one of five cereal grains (wheat, barley, oats, spelt, or rye) caused by its prolonged contact with water or other liquids. This prohibtion of Chometz on Pesach includes Chometz *Gomur* (unmixed Chometz) and *Ta'aruvas* Chometz (a mixture containing real Chometz).

There are 3 areas with which we must be concerned when evaluating Chometz. First, there is Isur Hana'ah, that is not deriving any pleasure or benefit whatsoever from the Chometz (e.g. feeding Chometz to your pets, etc.). Secondly, a Jew may not own Chometz. This prohibition extends to possession of Chometz anywhere in the world (such as in a boat, mountain retreat, etc.). Thirdly, there is a prohibition against having Chometz in our possession.We must be careful to remove all Chometz from our premises. We are not allowed to leave Chometz in our possession on Pesach even if we do not intend to use it, and we don't own it.

Bitul of Chometz: During the year, non-kosher ingredients that inadvertently become mixed with kosher ingredients may be halachically fit to eat. The reason for this leniency is that they are declared *"Batel Beshishim,"* (annulled in 60.) Thus if the quantity of kosher ingredients is more than sixty times that of the non-kosher ingredients, the kosher will nullify the non-kosher. This rule is true regarding Chometz on Pesach <u>only if the mixture was made before</u> Pesach. During Pesach, the laws of *"bitul"* are <u>not</u> applicable. In other words, during Pesach week, if even a tiny amount of Chometz falls into a large amount of kosher-for-Pesach food, it renders the food unfit for use on Pesach. As in all such halachic questions, a competent Rav should be consulted.

Consumption of Chometz: Since the prohibition of eating Chometz on Pesach applies not only to Chometz itself, but to any derivatives of Chometz or to any product that may contain Chometz, one should make certain that all food products that are bought for Pesach should have a certification by a reliable kashrus organization or orthodox rabbi.

Hana'ah (benefit) from Chometz: During Pesach we may not derive any sort of benefit from Chometz. It, therefore, may not be sold or used, even in business transactions or as pet food. Even some cosmetics must be Chometz free. Generally, there is no problem with the following products if they are not organic in nature and do not contain any grain by-products: baby cream, eyeliner, baby oil, acne aid, nail polish, talcum powder, mascara, stick powder deodorant, rouge (powder), Noxzema, petroleum jelly.

THE SEDER

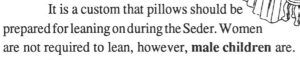

O ne should prepare everything for the Seder on Erev Pesach in order that the Seder should begin immediately upon arriving from Shul. This includes setting the table, etc.

It is a custom that pillows should be prepared for leaning on during the Seder. Women are not required to lean, however, **male children** are.

It is also a custom among some that the head of the household wears a *kittel* during the Seder.

In most places, the custom is that only the head of the household has a Seder plate and the 3 Matzos. Some, however, have a Seder plate and Matzos for each man present at the Seder. When only the head of the household has a Seder plate, he must provide for everyone at the Seder from his plate. Since there is usually not a sufficient amount of Matzos and *Marror* on the Seder plate for everyone, additional Matzo and *Marror* should be placed on the table for supplementary use. One should be certain to have enough Matzo, *Marror* and wine to enable everyone present (male and female) to eat and drink the required amounts during the Seder.

SELECTED LAWS AND CUSTOMS

O ne must not use Marror that was soaked for 24 hours or longer. Soaking this long can halachically be considered cooking and we must only use uncooked vegetables for Marror.

Charoses can be made of ground apples, pears, pomegranates, dates, figs, walnuts, almonds, ginger and cinnamon, to which wine is added.

Karpas is many vegetables upon which a bracho of "HaAdama" is made, is of the type to be dipped in salt water or vinegar,and is the type of vegetable which can be used on Pesach. Parsley, celery, and potatoes are often used as Karpas.

The **Zroa** is a piece of meat roasted over the fire. Most people use a chicken neck or wing for this purpose.

The **Baitza** is an ordinary hard-boiled or roasted egg. If one forgot to roast the Zroa or Baitzah on Erev Pesach and had to do it at night, he must eat it before sunset of the next day.

THE ARBAA KOSOS (FOUR CUPS OF WINE)

I t is preferable that the wine used at the Seder be red in color. For those who cannot drink wine, grape juice may be used. Nevertheless, one should make every effort to drink wine at the Seder. If necessary, wine and grape juice may be mixed.

The cups of wine should contain at least 3.3 fluid ounces. It is preferable to drink the entire cup, or at least half of it.

Men must consume all cups of wine while reclining on their left side. If one drank either of the first two cups without so reclining, he must drink it again without a brocho.

Caution: Tirosh Grape Juice with O/U is Kosher for Pesach, as is Kedem and other appropriately certified brands of grape juice. On the side of the bottle, it states in Hebrew that it can be used for fulfilling the Mitzvah of the four cups. Since not everyone may use grape juice instead of wine, we suggest that you consult your Rabbi as to when this would apply.

MATZO

O nly Matza Sh'mura (i.e. guarded Matza,) which is made of grain that has been guarded against fermentation from the time of harvest, should be used for the Seder. Both hand and machine Matzos Sh'mura are available. The consumption of Matza Ashira is prohibited for most people throughout Pesach. Matza Ashira is any Matza that contains products other than flour and water. Included in this category are: Matza which was kneaded with fruit juice, egg matza, tea matza, honey and spice matza and chocolate-covered matza. This prohibition, however, does not apply to infants or people who are ill.

EATING ON EREV PESACH

T he eating of Chometz is prohibited on Erev Pesach, from a third of the day and thereafter. In addition, it is forbidden to eat Matza on Erev Pesach. This prohibition includes cakes or cookies that are baked with matza meal. In order that the Matza at the Seder be eaten with a "hearty appetite", it is prohibited on Erev Pesach to eat anything that is baked with flour (i.e. matza farfel, etc.) Other foods should only be eaten in moderation from the ninth hour in the day on.

THE MITZVOS & WHEN THEY ARE DONE

MITZVAH	WHEN IT IS DONE	HOW MUCH	ALLOTED TIME (Preferably)
4 cups of wine	At appropriate times throughout the Seder	3.3 fluid oz., at least most of the cup. (each time)	Continuity with only 1 interuption
Matza	Motzi Matza and Afikoman (2 K'zeytim)	1/2 Machine Matza or 1/3 hand Matza	4 min.
	Korech (K'zayis)	1/4 Machine Matza or 1/6 hand Matza	2 min.
Marror (Horseradish) or	at "Al Achilas Marror"	1 fluid oz.	4 min.
Marror (Lettuce) or	at "Al Achilas Marror"	enough leaves to cover an area of 8"x10"	4 min.
Marror stalks)	at "Al Achilas Marror"	to cover area of 3"x5"	4 min.

91

KITNIYOS AND MATZA ASHIRA

Due to the stringency of not eating chometz on Pesach,Ashkenazic Jews have developed a custom not to eat Kitniyos (legumes) on Pesach. Kitniyos includes beans, rice, green beans, peas, millet, corn, mustard, lentils and lecithin. Many people refrain from eating peanuts, too. This restriction of peanuts however, does not include peanut oil (according to the opinion of Rav Moshe Feinstein ZT"L.)

Legumes are permitted for some Sephardic Jews who, for various historical reasons, did not adopt this custom of refraining from Kitniyos consumption on Pesach. This is why the kosher consumer is confronted yearly with a confusing array of *hechsherim* found on candies and jams, mustard and other products containing legumes. In reality, these products are usable on Pesach by only certain groups of people.

There is a similar problem concerning Matza Ashira, such as egg matza and chocolate covered egg matzas, which are only acceptable under certain conditions. Ashkenazic Jews, when doing their Pesach shopping, should be careful of products which contain corn oil, lecithin, glucose or emulsifiers, because these ingredients are often made from legumes.

According to reliable sources in England, the London Beis Din does not permit *kitniyos* in their products. However, since there are different opinions concerning lecithin, they do allow this ingredient in some of their products, including chocolate bars. The major Kashrus organizations in the U.S. do *not* allow lecithin in their products, and many products from abroad will state that no lecithin is included. One should not be confused by a candy called Intermezzo by Vered HaGalil - Rose of Galil bearing an O/U^P. This product contains lecithin from rape seed and not from soybean and, therefore is acceptable according to all standards.

Matza Ashira is made by mixing flour from one of the five grains with fruit juices or eggs, instead of water. *Matza Ashira* is permitted according to halacha for people who are sick and are otherwise unable to eat regular matza. This permitted group includes infants, the elderly, and the ill. In case of doubt, a rabbi should be consulted. Even one who is allowed to eat Matza Ashira, cannot fulfil the mitzvah of Achilas Matza with it.

"KOSHER STYLE" CERTIFICATIONS

I t has come to our attention that "kosher style" for Passover certifications are on the rise. In reality, the words "kosher style" are very misleading and border on being illegal. Federal law prohibits the direct falsification and/or misrepresentation of a non-kosher product as kosher. Unfortunately, this has not stopped many bogus "Passover" stickers from being used nor has it stopped some stores from intimating that something is kosher for Passover, when in fact it is **not.**

KASHERING UTENSILS

A ll utensils used for preparing food on Pesach must be kashered from the chometz that those utensils have absorbed when used during the rest of the year. Tablecloths and towels used year round should be washed thoroughly and may then be used for Pesach.

Surfaces upon which only cold chometz has been placed during the year, such as refrigerators and pantry shelves, should be thoroughly washed and rinsed to ready them for Pesach use. Surfaces which are used for hot chometz during the year, must, in addition, be kashered whenever possible, by pouring hot water on them and then covering with non-absorbent material, like contact paper, cardboard or aluminum foil.

To kasher an electric range, first scour it thoroughly. Then, turn on the highest temperature setting for 15 minutes, or until it gets red-hot. Enamel-glazed stove tops should be covered during Pesach. Gas grates should be put in the oven for kashering. The oven should be cleaned with a special solution, such as "Easy Off" and not used for 24 hours. After this time, it should be turned on to the maximum setting for one hour. This will kasher the oven but **not** the broiler. The broiler is difficult to kasher, therefore, it is usually not used for Pesach. If one desires to kasher it, *"Libbun"* (glowing hot) is required.

Many microwave ovens without browning elements can be kashered by first cleaning them, not using the oven for 24 hours and then putting new styrofoam or cardboard on the bottom. Self-cleaning ovens may be operated on the cleaning cycle and then used.

A stainless-steel sink is kashered by pouring boiling water over its entire surface after it has first been cleaned, and then kept free from hot water usage for 24 hours. Porcelain sinks, however, may not be kashered. They should be fully lined with a tin insert, or contact paper, or aluminum foil, and a Pesach inserted basin.

Metal utensils that are used with liquid (soup pots, etc.) can be kashered by first cleaning them, then not using them for 24 hours, and finally immersing them in a kashered pot full of boiling water for 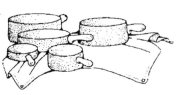 15 seconds, followed by rinsing them in cold water immediately upon removal.

Braces, bite plates and retainers should be brushed thoroughly before Pesach.

China, porcelain, "Corning Ware", plastic, stoneware, synthetics, synthetic rubber, melmac, pyrex, earthenware, and teflon-coated utensils cannot be kashered. These items should be washed well and put away until after Pesach.

MEDICINE

ost prescriptions can also be filled with Kosher-for-Pesach medicine. For information on the kosher status of your medicines contact the Kosher Information Bureau or your local reliable rabbi.

It has come to our attention that many U.S. companies have switched from synthetic alcohol to grain alcohol, as most of the synthetic alcohol now comes from Saudi Arabia. Extra caution is therefore necessary.

Since some prescriptions are, unfortunately, not available with Kosher certification, we will mention some guidelines for those who must take medicine on Pesach.

1. If someone suffers from an illness through which his life may become

endangered, he may eat chometz on Pesach and may use any medication needed to avoid a life threatening situation. This chometz should be owned by a non-Jew.

2.   If someone is ill, but his life is not endangered, he may not eat chometz on Pesach. However, he may take medicine under certain circumstances as long as he does not take it in the normal way. A Rabbi should be consulted if the need for such medicine should occur.

3.   Generally speaking, **cough syrups** and other liquid medicines may contain **grain alcohol** and may not be used on Pesach. When one must take medicine during Pesach, the doctor should be asked to prescribe medicine without alcohol or capsules.

Many common over-the-counter medicines require no special certification to be used on Pesach. They include (alphabetically):

KOSHER FOR PESACH
COMMON ITEMS WITH RELIABLE CERTIFICATION
(OR NOT REQUIRING PESACH CERTIFICATION ALTOGETHER*)

ITEM	BRAND (TYPE)
Alcohol	any Isopropyl or Synthetic(**not** grain-based alcohol)
Aluminum disposable containers	any brand
Aluminum foil	any brand
Ammonia	any brand
Baby formula	Similac, Enfamil, Prosobee, Soyalac, Isomil (in separate utensils as they contain kitniyos)
Baking soda (not baking powder)	any pure bicarbonate
Birdseed	natural sunflower seeds, millet
Bleach	any brand
Cocoa cocoa powder	Hershey's pure baking
Contact Lens Fluid	any brand
Dental floss	any unflavored brand

*as of the date of this publication — 1995

Frozen fruit	any plain (no sugar or syrup added)
Hairspray	any brand
Ice (from plain water)	any brand
Juices	any **brand name** unsweetened grade A frozen orange juice concentrate. Minute Maid 100% grapefruit concentrate. Citrus Hill or Tropicana Premium fresh juice in carton
Meats	most raw meats (<u>not</u> coated, processed, etc.) of reliable year-round *hechsher* are also kosher for Pesach. Check your local Rabbinic authority
Milk	any brand purchased **BEFORE** Pesach **only** from a company that does not process chocolate milk on the same machinery
Milk (dry)	Alba, Carnation
Mouthwash	Scope, Listerine
Nuts	any raw nut (even if bleached). Must be without BHA, BHT or other additives
Olive Oil	any olive oil from a Greek or Italian company which is extra-virgin

Paper Plates

Plastic ware, plastic coated paperware, styrofoam

Paper towels

any brand

Pepper

Morton's black pepper

Plastic bags & wraps

any brand - i.e., Saran Wrap, Reynolds Aluminum Foil, Glad Bags

Poultry

any reliable kosher brand that is not processed or coated (i.e., raw). Some popular brands are: Empire, Falls, Vineland,

Rice

for those **Sephardim** who use rice on Pesach, it is acceptable only without additives

Salt (coarse)

any brand

Scouring Pads

Dobie, Brillo Nylon Scrubber, Scotch Brite, Supreme, Chore Boy, Airwick Nylon, Golden Fleece, Rokeach Steel Wool Soap Pads

Seltzer (unflavored)

any brand

Shoe Polish

any brand

Soaps (hand)

any brand

Sugar (white)

any granulated pure **cane** sugar. This will be listed on the label. C&H, Domino , and Jack Frost are acceptable

Water (unflavored)   all

Water (flavored)   all Perrier flavors with O/KP

Vegetables   artichokes, asparagus, avocado, beets, bell peppers, broccoli, brussel sprouts, cabbage (red or green), carrots, cauliflower, celeriac (celery roots), celery, chicory, chives, collard, coriander (cilantro), cucumber, dandelion greens, dill, eggplant, endive, escarole, fennel (finnocio), garlic (depending on custom), green onions, horseradish (raw), kohlrabi, leek, lettuce (all types), mint leaves, mushrooms, okra, onions, potatoes, parsley, parsley root, pumpkin radishes (all types), rhubarb, rutabaga, scallions, spinach, tomatillos, tomatoes, turnips, watercress, whole pepper, yams, zucchini

INFORMATION BOOKLETS ABOUT PESACH

1   **Kosher Information Bureau**
     12753 Chandler Blvd., North Hollywood, CA 91607
     (818) 762-3197, FAX (818) 980-6908

     JFWS73A - Prodigy number
     Rabbi E. Eidlitz, Rabbinic Administrator

2.   **Medicines and Cosmetics of Pesach**
     by Rabbi Gershon Bess
     Kollel Los Angeles
     7466 Beverly Blvd., Los Angeles, CA 90036
     (213) 933-7193 (leave name and address on answering machine)

3.   **Vaad Hakashrus of Baltimore - Kashrus Kurrents**
     7504 Seven Mile Lane, Baltimore, MD 21208
     (410) 484-4110

4.   **Kashrus Newsletter from Birkas Reuven** (Rabbi Yosef Winkler)
     P.O. Box 204, Brooklyn, NY 11204
     (718) 998-3201

PRODUCTS TO BE CAUTIOUS OF FOR PESACH USE

ITEM	PROBLEMS
Apple juice	Nutrients (sometimes vinegar equipment), enzymes, clarifying agents.
Applesauce	corn syrup, sugar, dextrose
Baby cereals and food	can contain wheat, sugar, and be made on Chometz equipment
Bird food	many contain grain
Brown sugar	culture, yeast (can even have wheat starch)
Butter	salt, coloring, preservatives, nutrients, culture, lactic acid from corn
Candied fruits	dextrose (can have powdered sugar or flour)
Canned & frozen fruits & Vegetables with Syrup	may be iodized with flour, dextrose (di – etetic may contain grape juice in syrup)
Cat food	wheat, meat, cheese, whey, oats and barley
Canned fruits	corn syrup
Cheese and cottage cheese	stabilizers & corn sugar, coagulating agent microbial rennet from real chometz, stabilizer, dextrose, cultures

Chewing gum flavoring	corn syrup and flavoring
Chocolate & chocolate milk	malt (real chometz) and glucose
Cider vinegar	may contain yeast that is real chometz
Cocoa	can be made on chometz equipment
Coffee	
	General Foods International currently is processed on chometz machinery some contain grain, such as Postum
Decaffeinated coffee	may have been processed with ethyl acetate derived from grain alcohol
Coffee, flavored	may contain chometz alcohol as well as non-kosher flavoring
Condensed milk	sugar and preservatives (oil to reconstitute)
Confectionery sugar	corn starch (for instance, 3% in C&H) and sometimes wheat starch
Creamer, non dairy	whey and emulsifiers which are dairy and kitniyos, some contain corn syrup
Dishwashing detergent	cetyl alcohol (not kosher) and grain alcohol
Dextrose	corn derivative
Dog food	barley, oats, wheat, cheese, whey and meat
Dried fruits and raisins	dried in chometz ovens: sometimes sprayed with kitniyos oil

Emulsifiers	can contain glucose
Fish food	wheat
Flour	has been bleached and washed, therefore chometz
Frozen fruit drinks	usually contain corn syrup
Gelatin	from all over the world, including Israel, not acceptable
Glucose	corn derivative
Honey	corn syrup and coloring (even when not listed)
Horseradish	vinegar and sweeteners
Hydrolyzed Vegetable Protein	Wheat Gluten
Ice cream	sugar, flavorings and stabilizers
Ketchup	stabilizers, oil, dextrose, vinegar (real chometz), flavorings
Lecithin	kitniyos
Liquors	may have grain alcohol base, wine, or grain alcohol, or wine alcohol
Oil	kitniyos
MSG	wheat

Margarine	emulsifiers, artificial flavor, salt, sugar, oil
Maraschino cherries	glucose, dextrose
Mayonnaise	MSG from hydrolyzed protein, oil, flavorings, sweeteners, vinegar
Milk	must be bought before Pesach and processed by a dairy that does not make chocolate milk (see section on milk)
Nuts	BHA, BHT, sprayed in kitniyos (corn oil)
Paper plates (inexpensive)	coated with starch
Peanuts	considered kitniyos
Powdered cocoa	powdered milk, corn sweetener
Pet food	wheat, milk & meat together. (meat and cheese, or whey, - not acceptable all year)
Pickles	vinegar and flavorings
Play dough	wheat (must be discarded before Pesach)
Processed or flavored spices	dextrose and flavorings
Products from Rabbanut of Israel or England	may contain kitnyos
Rice	Ashkenazim do not use rice on Pesach It is kitniyos
Salt	table salt often contains dextrose and polysorbate especially when iodized

Soda	flavorings, dextrose, corn sugar
Soy oil, corn oil, corn syrup, soy lecithin	all are Kitniyos
Tofu	made from soy bean
Tomato products	vinegar (chometz) nutrients, salt, sugar
Tuna	hydrolyzed protein and oil
Vanilla extract	corn syrup, alcohol
Vitamins	yeast, starch and corn dextrose, wheat
Wine	corn sugar, alcohol
Yogurt	milk powder enzymes and sugar

FROZEN VEGETABLES

A new problem has arisen concerning using frozen vegetables for Pesach. Most large companies, such as S&W, Green Giant, Bird's Eye, etc. purchase their vegetables from many different processors. Due to increased competition in this industry from Mexico and Guatemala, many packers have begun processing pasta and vegetables in their blanching equipment when it is not in use for pure vegetables. This is done at temperatures between 100 and 200 degrees, thus making the machinery unacceptable for Pesach use. Some companies are introducing steam-blanchers which are not usable for pasta. This may help in the future.

MECHIRAS (SELLING OF) CHOMETZ

Mechiras Chometz is the sale of Jewish-owned chometz to a non-Jew before Pesach. We must sell chometz that is in our regular homes, vacation homes, etc. This transfer of chometz to a non-Jew is a legal and binding sale, complete with contract. This sale is transacted through a Rabbi, who acts as an agent to sell the Jew's chometz to a non-Jew. The Rabbi enters into an agreement with the non-Jew for the sale of this chometz. The chometz that has been sold must be placed in a totally sealed-off area, and must remain there throughout the holiday of Pesach.

SODA

In determining whether a type of soda is kosher for Pesach, there are three major ingredients that we are concerned with: brominated vegetable oil, flavorings and sugar. Corn syrup, which is made from kitniyos, is a common sweetener in soda. The other ingredient, "flavoring", is also a source of concern. Generally speaking, flavoring is the key to a product's success in the food market. Its formula is, therefore, a highly guarded secret of the company. Even a minuscule change in the formula of a product where flavoring is concerned can prove to be disastrous, as in the case of Coca Cola. It is not surprising, then, that these companies guard these flavorings very carefully. Only recently has Coke, for instance, allowed access to their formula. The general public would not be privy to this kind of information and, therefore, a mashgiach is necessary to go to the plant to personally check the flavorings being used. It is also important to note that even within the same company (Coke, Pepsi, etc.), each individual bottling plant throughout the country may choose to use corn syrup as a sweetener. For this reason as well, it is essential that a reliable mashgiach be on the premises during production.

There are thousands of flavorings used by the food industry, not all of which are kosher (let alone for Pesach). Some, such as ambergris (from whale intestines) and civit absolute (from cats) are, of course, not kosher. Even when we know that a soda is reliably certified kosher in a particular city, this does not mean that the same brand of soda is kosher elsewhere. Each region of the country has its own bottling plants which therefore require their own local hashgachas.

EGGS

It is best to buy eggs that were laid before Pesach. Since chickens are fed chometz on Pesach, there is a *minhag* not to eat eggs laid on Pesach.

RICE

Ashkenazim do not eat rice during Pesach. Those Sephardim whose *minhag* permits them to eat rice on Pesach must be careful to determine that the rice is additive-free. (This includes vitamins.) Additive-free rice can be purchased in many health food stores. The tradition among Sephardim is to check the rice 3 times for Chometz. In any case open bins should not be used.

MILK

Due to the modern pasteurizing processes used in the milk industry, many nutrients are removed. Governmental regulations dictate that Vitamin D and in some cases, Vitamin A be added to milk before its sale. The amounts added are very minute. Inasmuch as that Vitamins A and D are often derived from chometz or *kitniyos* and since mixtures of even small amounts of chometz on Pesach are **not** *"batel"* (annulled), we must be careful about these additives.

Another matter of concern is the processing equipment. Milk companies often produce chocolate milk on the same equipment that they use for their "white" milk. The chocolate milk can contain malt, which is made from grain. In order to avoid these problems, two steps are necessary. First, it is necessary to make sure that the dairy company whose milk we purchase for Pesach only processes "white" milk and not chocolate milk. Secondly, the milk that we need for all of Pesach must be bought **before** Pesach. By doing this, the vitamins in the milk were deemed *"batel"* from before Pesach and therefore may be used on Pesach. Whenever possible, certified kosher-for-Passover milk is preferable.

MARSHMALLOWS AND GELATINS

Although many Kosher-for-Passover marshmallows are presumably made without chometz ingredients, they nevertheless can contain a highly controversial ingredient: gelatin. The main sources of gelatin are cattle and hogs. The collagen in the bones and skin of these animals is converted by soaking 2"x3" strips of hide in hydrochloric acid until it turns into ossein. This is then soaked in lime for about a month, and then it is washed in sulfuric acid to obtain the gelatin. In 1912, Rav Chaim Ozer Grodzenski ZT"L sent a response to the Royal Gelatin Company concerning the methods of obtaining kosher gelatin from non-kosher hides. In 1950, Rav Lazer Silver vehemently opposed the hechsher on a well-known gelatin product. In 1966, Rav Moshe Feinstein ZT"L, and Rav Aaron Kotler ZT"L opposed all gelatins that were not obtained from a kosher source. Kosher gelatin, from kosher slaughtered animals, tends to be too expensive for most companies to produce. This is the reason that the O/U, O/K and other reliable certifying agencies insist on a gelatin substitute in products needing gelatin, or on a reliably cerifier gelatin. Marshmallows are a prime example of such a product. Some acceptable substitutes for gelatin are: Japanese gelatin, Japanese insinglass, agar agar, Chinese moss, Irish moss, carrageenan. However, there is a new type of fish gel that is being used in pharmaceuticals and this may prove in the future to be a better substitute for gelatin. Currently, kosher gelatin from kosher hides is being produced under reliable supervision and is marketed under the brand name "Kolatin". (See page 191)

CHOMETZ SHE'AVAR ALAV HAPESACH
(BUYING CHOMETZ AFTER PESACH)

Due to the severity of the "Issur" (prohibition) of chometz, Chazal reinforced the sale of chometz with a fine. The form of this fine was levied on any Jew who kept chometz in his possession or ownership. This is called "Chometz She'avar Alav HaPesach"

The law requires that if a Jew owns chometz on Pesach, no Jew is allowed to eat that food even after Pesach. We are therefore also prohibited from buying from stores that are Jewish owned, if they have not sold their chometz.

Rav Moshe Feinstein ZT"L in his *sefer Igros Moshe*, states that if a Jew sold his chometz for Pesach and then kept his store open during Pesach and continued to sell items of chometz, we are nevertheless allowed to buy from that store after Pesach.

FOR FURTHER KASHRUS INFORMATION HOTLINES

CITY	RABBI	PHONE
Baltimore	Rabbi Moshe Heineman - Star K	(410) 484-4110
Chicago	Rabbi Chaim Goldszweig - O/U	(312) 764-5322
Detroit	Rabbi Beryl Broyde - Merkaz	(313) 559-5005
Los Angeles	Rabbi Yehuda Bukspan	(213) 653-5083
Los Angeles	Rabbi Aryeh Weiner - O/U	(310) 965-9125
Los Angeles	K.I.B. Kosher Info. Bureau Hotline	(818) 762-3197
Los Angeles	R.C.C., Rabbi Union	(310) 271-4160
Northridge	Rabbi Aharon Simkin	(818) 368-2254
New York	Rabbi Don Yoel Levy - O/K	(718) 756-7500
New York	O/U Kosher Hotline	(212) 563-4000

OILS

I n the last few decades, there has been a sharp worldwide decline in the use of animal oils. Between 1970 and 1975 the use of animal oils decreased by 39 percent, and the use of marine oil decreased 24 percent. In fact, by 1975, more than two-thirds of the world's food oil needs were met by vegetable oils.

These figures should not, however, be construed to indicate corresponding increases and decreases in the United States. In actuality, there has been an increase in lard and tallow (beef fat) use in the U.S. The reasons for this are, first, that it is cheaper, due to a more active consumption in this country of animals as food, with a corresponding increase in the use of animal by-products, and, second, the superior shortening qualities of animal fats.

The biggest problem for the kosher consumer occurs because oil processors produce both animal and vegetable oils on the same equipment. This is particularly problematic in the case of hydrogenated (hardened) oils. Many of today's vegetable oils are hydrogenated in order to harden them. The oil is first heated to 250 degrees Fahrenheit in a vacuum (usually in the same equipment used for animal oils). A solid catalyst, which may be non-kosher based, is then added, and hydrogen gas is applied under pressure.

The exception to this is extra virgin olive oil, which has been processed using a cold press method. In this way, the oil is never heated and does not come in contact with any non-kosher oils.

The implications for the kosher consumer are clear. Most vegetable oils and products produced from them, such as margarine and shortening, cannot be relied on as kosher without strict rabbinic supervision.

EGGS

A basic rule of kashrus is that the product of a non-kosher animal is not kosher. Therefore, all eggs from non-kosher birds (and non-kosher fish and animals, such as turtles,) are not kosher.

To be kosher, eggs must come from kosher fowl and be free of bloodspots in the white (albumin) and the yolk. Each egg must be checked individually after it is opened. If there is blood in an egg, it is forbidden.

Eggs from a chicken that died are forbidden by rabbinic enactment.

If eggs are found in a chicken after shechita, they are considered meat and need to be kashered. (They should be soaked and salted by themselves.)

If an egg containing an embryo is cooked together with other eggs, none of the eggs are kosher.

1. Blood Spots:
   a. If the blood is in the kesher-knot, it is forbidden by the Torah.
   b. If there is blood in any egg, it is forbidden.
   Today most eggs are non-fertilized and are not forbidden from the Torah.

2. The Halacha says there are two ways to identify a kosher egg. It will have one side round and one side pointed and a yolk inside with white around it.

Fortified eggs - means eggs that have extra yolk added to them. Eggs are used in many foods. Some are:

   a. Pasta: Egg white for a binder and yolk for color.

111

b. Ice cream: egg yolk for color (all natural yellow vanilla)
c. French ice cream : frozen custard must have at least 2.8 percent egg yolk.
d. Egg Albumin: stabilizer, thickener, texturizer, in baked goods, candies, fruit drinks, frostings, mayonnaise, baked goods.

Reb Moshe Feinstein, ZT"L states the following concerning unfertilized eggs: "Concerning eggs that are unfertilized, only the blood spot within them would have to be removed, not the whole egg. Of concern, I spoke to a farmer who told me that deals in fertilized and unfertilized eggs... and when he has an overabundance of fertilized eggs, he adds them to the unfertilized eggs for sale in supermarkets. However, it is clear that not too many farmers do this, and those who do only do so with a few eggs." Therefore, if one buys an egg from the store in the United States, it can be considered a kosher egg, even without checking it. However, it is common custom to check all eggs for bloodspots and to treat them as if they were fertilized.

(Though this is the actual Halacha, since many rabbis have been very strict in this regard, it is good not to be lenient with eggs. Therefore, if a person knows that eggs are being purchased from a farmer who raises both fertilized and unfertilized eggs, even though they are probably unfertilized, we tend to be strict. On the other hand, if two eggs from the supermarket are cooked together in one pot, even if the larger egg is found to have a bloodspot, we only need to remove the egg with the bloodspot and the other one can be eaten. The exception to this is if the bloodspot is in the yolk *and* the white part of the egg (which is very rare). In that case, we tend to be even stricter. (Synopsis of responsa from Rav Moshe Feinstein on eggs.)

EGG SUBSTITUTES

 wo types of egg substitutes are available, one for the general public and the other for commercial use by bakeries.

The general public can purchase an egg substitute made from egg whites, vegetable oil, nonfat dry milk, emulsifiers, and artificial flavors and colors. Such products present no problems to certification agencies if the individual ingredients are kosher. If a certified version of these products can be found, the kosher consumer will find them excellent for making scrambled eggs and as substitutes for fresh eggs in recipes. It is for the latter use that commercial bakeries purchase egg substitutes.

An extract of cod or haddock (both kosher fish) can be used to make a "substitute egg white." A derived protein from skim milk, can be used like the fish protein as a powdered egg (see albumin) substitute. These two egg substitutes can theoretically be produced under kosher supervision, although the halacha opposes the introduction of dairy products into breads. A third source of egg substitutes is plasma obtained from blood. This substance would render any product in which it is found not kosher.

Food producers also use frozen or powdered eggs instead of whole fresh eggs. These must be certified kosher since there is a real possibility that eggs from a non-kosher species may be added, especially if cheaper, imported eggs are used. The Japanese have a large market for frozen and powdered eggs in this country. Therefore, products listing powdered or frozen eggs as ingredients must have supervision.

Another cheaper substitute for fresh whole eggs is the ova, the egg found in a hen after slaughter. Due to the fact that these are non-kosher eggs, they present a serious kashrus problem. Although a blood spot renders the egg not kosher, governmental regulations require only the removal of the blood, not the disposal of the egg itself. It is important for the kosher consumer to realize that in this area, the government is more lenient than Jewish law.

HEALTH FOODS

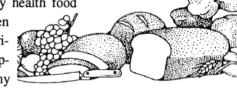

illions of Americans, many of them adhering to a kosher diet, have turned away from the synthetic, processed foods dominating supermarket shelves to the natural foods offered by health food stores. Although people often succeed in finding more nutritious food, they are often disappointed at not finding as many kosher products as they had anticipated in these health food stores. Fortunately, these kosher certified products are on the rise now.

Health food stores typically carry a large assortment of nutrition supplements, many of which are inherently kosher and need no certification. Products such as kelp, brewers yeast, most olive oils, raw nuts, sea salt, etc. need no *hechsher* (certifying mark) and can be readily purchased at any health food store.

A snap judgment might be made that "natural health foods" are largely faddist foods and, therefore, not worthy of the kosher consumer's attention. However, such a judgement would be unfair. The dictionary defines "fad" as something in which many people are interested in for a short period of time. Since many natural "health foods" are mentioned in the Talmud, and interest in them has continued to this day, health foods certainly cannot be defined as a fad!

Two popular myths among health food advocates, however, are that "natural" is necessarily healthy and automatically kosher. We can even find people who adhere to the strictest kosher observance at home, and yet feel that eating cooked fish or other natural foods in a health food restaurant is in accordance with Jewish law. Nothing is further from the truth.

Let us examine the term "natural" to better understand its implications for kashrus and health. "Natural" only means "an unadulterated state." This would include non-kosher fish or oils processed from animals. Strictly speaking, even flavorings such as coumarin (from the tonka bean) or oil of calamus, which are very dangerous to the consumer, would come under the category of "natural" foods. Of course, these last mentioned are banned by the F.D.A. and will not be found in any stores. On the other hand, non-kosher grape juice, cochineal, (from beetles) and civet (from the civet cat) may definitely be found in various foods carried by health food stores.

As with other foods, health foods fall into 3 categories: foods which cannot be kosher; foods which can be kosher with proper inspection and certification; and foods which are kosher even without certification. Just as the F.D.A. has banned some natural foods from public use because they are harmful, we kosher consumers must be aware of which natural foods to ban from our own diets. There is a need for kosher certification on most health foods, as on other foods. On the other hand, it is easier to determine if something is kosher if there are no hidden ingredients. For example, natural peanut butter in most cases needs no hechsher since it is made entirely from peanuts.

ISRAELI FOODS

O ne might think that food from Israel is automatically kosher, and the fact that Hebrew writing is on the label tends to lend credence to that belief. Unfortunately, food grown in Israel presents more problems for the kosher consumer than does food grown outside of Israel. As a result, the general rule is that no Israeli food can be eaten without acceptable rabbinic supervision.

The additional stringencies that apply to food grown in Israel are of two kinds, "periodic" and "constant". The two "periodic" problems arise from the laws of *Orlah* and *Shmittah*. Orlah (literally, "uncircumcised") is the Torah's designation for fruit from trees and grapevines during the first 3 years following the planting or replanting of the tree. Such fruit is forbidden for consumption. In the fourth year from (re)planting, the fruit is called *Neta'-reva'i* ("fourth year planting") and can be eaten, but only after it is properly redeemed by the owner.

The laws of *Orlah* and *Neta' reva'i* also apply to trees outside of Israel and to backyard fruit trees most specifically. The assumption is that supermarket produce outside of Israel is free of orlah or neta' reva'i whereas Israeli produce must be carefully supervised to insure that these laws are kept.

The second type of periodic problem arises from *Shmittah*, the Torah injunction to allow the land of Israel to lie fallow every seventh year. This sabbatical year is subject to numerous laws that govern planting and harvesting, and only food produced in accordance with those laws is permissible for eating. An additional complication has recently arisen with a rabbinic dispensation that allows selling Jewish land to (trustworthy) non-Jews for the duration of the *Shmittah*. The consumer must know that although some supervising rabbis in Israel rely on this dispensation, it has not received general acceptance by leading rabbinic authorities. It is therefore possible that a local rabbi will deem as "not kosher" a product approved by a chief rabbi in Israel. This indicates the rabbi's concern that the food may contain sabbatical year produce.

Some fruits even purchased outside of Israel, could well be forbidden as *Shmittah* produce. Processed fruits and vegetables (such as canned produce, jellies, dried fruits, fruited ice creams and yogurt), grain products (including baked goods), and spices require supervision for assurance that no sabbatical year produce has been used.

The stringencies that are constant on Israeli food all stem from the Torah's system of tithes required from a farmer's produce. These include a 2 percent donation to the priests (called *Terumah)* and a 10 percent donation from the balance of the crop to the Levites *(Ma' aser Rishon* or "First Tithe"). Approximately 10 percent of produce is stockpiled for the owner to eat in Jerusalem (Ma'aser Sheni, "Second Tithe"). In the third and sixth years of the seven-year *Shmittah* cycle, the *Ma' aser Oni* was distributed among the poor. Each year the Levite was expected to give 10 percent of the tithe he received to the priests, and this amount (1 percent of the farmer's original crop) was called *Terumas Ma' aser* ("the priest's portion from the tithe"). All produce grown in Israel is subject to these provisions, and only after tithes takes place may the produce be eaten.

T'nuva, the umbrella cooperative for Israeli farmers, does take out the requisite portion in Israel, but not for their export crop. Therefore, fresh produce offered for sale in stores in Israel is not *Vadai Tevel* ("certainly untithed"). But because *tevel* ("untithed produce") may have become mixed before retailing, the produce is considered *demai* ("possibly untithed produce"), and the tithes are therefore taken without a blessing being recited. There are many stores where the necessary tithes are separated under the supervision of the Bais Din Tzedek. The stores display a sign reading "Produce from this store is ready to eat" under supervision of the Badatz.

Climatic conditions and the minimal use of insecticides in Israel present a real possibility of finding insects and worms in produce, including dried produce. When possible, one should inspect produce before eating it. Processed food, however, must bear notices of appropriate rabbinic supervision. There are a few organizations whose supervision can always be assumed reliable with regard to the special requirements applicable to Israeli produce. Some of them are:

1) The familiar O/U.

2) The Bais Din Tzedek ("true court") of the Eidah Haharedis of Jerusalem, popularly known as the *BaDaTz*. Their symbol can be found on a variety of packaged and processed products, as well as in bakeries, falafel shops, produce stores, and restaurants in Jerusalem. The symbol may be very small on a package or faintly stamped onto the package label with an ink pad.

3) The *Hug Hasam Sofer* of Bnei Brak. Their symbol is found often on dairy products, such as cheese, yogurts (called Preegurt in Israel), and ice cream. Since the emblem is embossed on the foil lids of yogurt, it can easily be missed.

4) Rabbi Moshe Landau (or Lande), of Bnei Brak. The notice of Rabbi Landau's supervision usually appears on the side panel or back of the package. Products under his supervision include candies, cold cuts, smoked meats, ice cream (both dairy and pareve), and many Osem brand products. (Note: Not all Osem products are supervised, and some even state "Not for those who observe the sabbatical year laws." One must read each label carefully.)

5) The Belz Community. This supervision symbol is appearing increasingly on a variety of packaged products, including canned goods, cookies, etc. This emblem, too, often appears very small or simply stamped on, ink-pad fashion.

6) The Agudas Yisrael's emblem is found in the beginning of this book. A notice of their supervision usually appear clearly on labels of products ranging from canned goods and cheeses to other dairy products. It can be

found embossed on the foil lids of yogurt containers.

The chief rabbinates of various cities may accept dispensations not accepted by most leading authorities. Their supervision is not always sufficient. Therefore, a competent authority must be consulted.

Most Israeli restaurants, bakeries, ice cream shops, pizza and falafel stands, etc. bear a prominently displayed certificate of kashrus *(te'udas kashrus)*. Only a few are from one of the above approved organizations. One must carefully check out establishments with only local Israeli supervision before eating in them. As is true in the United States, the best rule is, "When in doubt, go without."

Restaurants

"Eating out" is easy in a city blessed with kosher restaurants under reliable supervision. But where there are no kosher restaurants, many people who otherwise are very careful about kashrus observance at home succumb to the temptation of eating in a non-kosher restaurant. They rely on the common myth that many foods do not require supervision and can be eaten in any restaurant.

We have already discussed in some detail that neither "health foods" nor "natural foods" are intrinsically kosher. The same is true with health-food restaurants. Even in ordinary restaurants, one often sees Orthodox people enjoying a nice dinner with apparent ease. However, if we examine a menu from either type of restaurant, we will find very little that can truly be ordered without risk of eating *treif*. A typical breakfast may consist of coffee, fried or hardboiled eggs, or lox and bagels with cream cheese. *Some* of the problems with these foods could be as follows:

1) unflavored coffee   none, if served in a kosher cup, without cream.

2) fried eggs   non-kosher frying pan; non-kosher oil or margarine; non-kosher eggs.

3) hardboiled eggs   non-kosher eggs; non-kosher boiling pot (shell is permeable).

4) lox   cured with non-kosher fish.

5) bagels   shortening (non-kosher); di-glycerides; non-kosher release agents; non-kosher egg substitutes, non-kosher equipment.

6) cream cheese   non-kosher rennet and culture.

If one chose dinner in a non-kosher restaurant and ordered fish, cole slaw, salad, orange juice, mustard or ketchup, with a side dish of pure cooked beans, the following problems could be present:

1) tuna fish   non-kosher oil, unsupervised packing.

2) cooked fish   non-kosher oil for cooking; non-kosher sea-
                    sonings; frying pan used for non-kosher
                    food; inability to determine if fish is truly from
                    kosher species.

3) orange juice   none.

4) cole slaw   bugs (prevalent in cabbage); dressings with oils,
                    emulsifiers, oil, oxystearin, etc.

5) salad   radishes, onions cut with *treif* cutlery; non-kosher
                    dressing.

6) mustard   oleoresins; turmeric (containing emulsifiers
                    and glycerides).

7) ketchup   processing equipment; same as mustard.

8) beans   processed on ham and pork equipment cooked in
                    non-kosher utensils.

In all of these cases, we must remember that any kosher food that is boiled, baked, grilled, fried or broiled in a treif utensil previously used for non-kosher products or for meat and dairy products indiscriminately will itself be non-kosher, and should not be eaten. Furthermore, any kosher food, when served hot on a non-kosher dish is rendered non-kosher.

What is permissible in a non-kosher restaurant is: coffee or tea prepared in a special, separate utensil and served in styrofoam cups; cold fruit or salad, which were cut with a permissible knife and served on cold, clean non-kosher utensils. Unfortunately, even this can prove to be a disappointing experience, as many waiters and chefs add sauces, dressings or cottage cheese to salads, even when not requested to do so. The Kosher patron should always be certain to tell the waiter that the salad should be served without any dressings or chef's' surprises (e.g., salami cubes, bacon strips, etc.).

Another matter of concern to the Kosher patron who considers eating even something innocuous (such as a soft drink) at, say, Mc Donald's is the serious problem of *"ma'aris ayin"*, the "appearance to the eye." People who don't know better may reach the wrong conclusion about the status of eating anything in such an establishment, or about your personal practice.

On the other hand, airline meals that are served in their own container, may avoid the problem of *"ma'aris ayin."* This is why people eat these types of meals on airlines, Disneyland (as of this publication), hotels, etc. However, even in these cases, care must be taken that the meal will remain double-wrapped when it is heated and served and that only plastic or kosher cutlery be used.

In conclusion, it is evident that kashrus observance deserves the same care and caution wherever one eats, whether in restaurants or at home.

FOOD ADDITIVES

 ood additives are any substances used in producing, manufacturing, packing, processing, preparing, treating, packaging, transporting, or holding food. There are 3 different types of additives: intentional, incidental, and chance.

Intentional additives are actual ingredients, and these usually must be indicated in some manner on the label. There are some cases in which the label can be misleading. Some ingredients can be lumped together rather than listed individually. There are ingredients which cannot be readily identified. Acetone-3-hydroxy-3-butanone, though it may sound formidable, is one of the characteristic flavoring elements in margarine and is generally not named. Of course, neither poisonous methanol (wood alcohol) nor acetone (paint remover) is identified as a natural component of coffee, which contains over 250 separately identifiable chemicals, many of which are considered toxic when ingested individually.

Manufacturers have also received permission to substitute such names as "artificial smoke flavor" for "pyroligenous acid." Incidental additives are included by the manufacturer as a food component. For example, the oil in which fish fillets are fried is an incidental additive, as are the anti-oxidants in that oil. Incidental additives often need not be listed on the label. Therefore, they present a problem for the kosher consumer.

Chance additives, including contaminants that get into food accidentally, pesticides from produce, hormones from meat and poultry, antibiotics, and processing aids such as release agents are certainly not listed on labels. These also may present special problems for the kosher consumer.

Thirty-two functions of additives are recognized in Federal regulations. More than two-thirds of these functions can be performed by both kosher and non-kosher additives. Care is required, therefore— the label can hide as much as it reveals.

CATEGORIES OF ADDITIVE FUNCTIONS
AS USED IN THE REGULATION OF FOOD INGREDIENTS

1. **Anti-caking agents and free-flow agents:** Substances added to finely powdered or crystalline food products to prevent caking, lumping, or agglomeration.

2. **Anti-microbial agents:** Substances used to preserve food by preventing growth of microorganisms and subsequent spoilage, including fungistats, mold and rot inhibitors, and the effects listed by the National Academy of Sciences/National Research Council under "preservatives".

3. **Anti-oxidants:** Substances used to preserve food by retarding deterioration, rancidity, or discoloration due to oxidation.

4. **Colors and coloring adjuncts:** Substances used to impart, preserve, or enhance the color or shading of a food, including color stabilizers, color fixatives, color-retention agents, etc.

5. **Curing and pickling agents:** Substances imparting a unique flavor and/or color to a food, usually producing an increase in shelflife stability.

6. **Dough strengtheners:** Substances used to modify starch and gluten, thereby producing a more stable dough, including the applicable effects listed by the National Academy of Sciences/National Research Council under "dough conditioners."

7. **Drying agents:** Substances with moisture-absorbing ability, used to maintain an environment of low moisture.

8. **Emulsifiers and emulsifier salts:** Substances that modify surface tension in the component phase of an emulsion to establish a uniform dispersion or emulsion.

9. **Enzymes:** Enzymes used to improve food processing and the quality of the finished food.

10. **Firming agents:** Substances added to precipitate residual pectin thus strengthening the supporting tissue and preventing its collapse during processing.

11. **Flavor enhancers:** Substances added to supplement, enhance, or modify the original taste and/or aroma of a food, without imparting a characteristic taste or aroma of its own.

12. **Flavoring agents and adjuvants:** Substances added to impart or help impart a taste or aroma in food.

13. **Flour-treating agents:** Substances added to milled flour, at the mill, to improve its color and/or baking qualities, including bleaching and maturing agents.

14. **Formulation aids:** Substances used to promote or produce a desired physical state or texture in food, including carriers, binders, fillers, plasticizers, film-formers, and tableting aids.

15. **Fumigants:** Volatile substances used for controlling insects or pests.

16. **Humecants:** Hydroscopic substances incorporated in food to promote retention of moisture, including moisture-retention agents and anti-dusting agents.

17. **Leavening agents:** Substances used to produce or stimulate production of carbon dioxide in baked goods to impart a light texture, including yeast, yeast foods, and calcium salts listed by the National Academy of Sciences/National Research Council under "dough conditioners".

18. Lubricants and release agents: Substances added to food contact surfaces and to food to prevent ingredients and finished products from sticking to them.

19. Non-nutritive sweeteners: Substances having less than 2% of the caloric value of sucrose per equivalent unit of sweetening capacity.

20. Nutrient supplements: Substances necessary for the body's nutritional and metabolic processes.

21. Nutritive sweeteners: Substances having greater than 2% of the caloric value of sucrose per equivalent unit of sweetening capacity.

22. Oxidizing and reducing agents: Substances that chemically oxidize or reduce another food ingredient, thereby producing a more stable product, including the applicable effect listed by the National Academy of Sciences/National Research Council under "dough conditioners."

23. pH Control agents: Substances added to change or maintain active acidity or basicity, including buffers, acids, alkalies, and neutralizing agents.

24. Processing aids: Substances used as manufacturing aids to enhance the appeal or utility of a food or food component, including clarifying agents, clouding agents, catalysts, flocculents, filter aids, and crystallization inhibitors.

25. Propellants, seating agents, and gases: Gases used to supply force to expel a product or used to reduce the amount of oxygen in contact with the food packaging.

26. Sequestrants: Substances that combine with polyvalent metalions to form a soluble metal complex, to improve the quality and stability of products.

27. **Solvents and vehicles:** substances used to extract or dissolve another substance.

28. **Stabilizers and thickeners:** Substances used to produce viscous solutions or dispersions, to impart body, improve consistency, or stabilize emulsions, including suspending and bodying agents, setting agents, jellying agents, bulking agents, etc.

29. **Surface-active agents:** Substances used to modify surface properties of liquid food components for a variety of effects, other than emulsifiers, but including solubilizing agents, dispersants, detergents, wetting agents, rehydration enhancers, whipping agents, foaming agents, and defoaming agents.

30. **Surface-finishing agents:** Substances used to increase palatability, preserve gloss, and inhibit discoloration of foods, including glazes, polishes, waxes, and protective coatings.

31. **Synergists:** Substances used to act or react with another food ingredient to produce a total effect different from or greater than the sum of the effects produced by the individual ingredients.

32. **Texturizers:** Substances that affect the appearance or feel of the food.

SOURCE: Federal Register, September 23, 1974, pp. 34173-34176.

INGREDIENTS AND THEIR USES

Acetic Acid - is found in plant juices, milk, oil, petroleum and sometimes muscles. It is the final product of many aerobic fermentations. When it is from petroleum, it is **kosher, pareve with supervision.**

Agar Agar - Source: seaweed. Use: a substitute for gelatin (cream and in confectionery items). **Kosher, pareve without supervision.**

Albumin - Sources: blood (serum albumin), milk (dairy), eggs. Use: Coagulant and stiffener in baked goods. **Requires supervision.**

Alginates - Source: seaweed. Forms: calcium alginate, alginic acid, sodium alginate, propylene glycol aginate. Uses: thickening and stabilizing agent in pastry, jelly, ice cream, cheese, candy, yogurt, canned frosting, whipped cream, and beer. **Kosher, pareve without supervision.**

Alginic Acid - See Alginates.

Alpha Amylase - Source: hog pancreas. Use: in flour to break down any starches. **Not Kosher.**

Alum Aluminum Sulfate - Source: earth. Also known as cake alum or patent alum. Use: clarifying oils and fats. **Kosher, pareve without supervision.**

Ambergris - Source: whale intestines. Use: flavoring (also used in perfume). **Not Kosher.**

Anise - Source: fruit of an herb (in the parsley family). Use: flavoring foods and beverages. **Kosher, pareve without supervision.**

Argol - Source: sediment in wine casks during fermentation and storage. Use: in the manufacture of tartaric acid and vinegar from malt. See also Cream of tartar and tartaric acid.

Ascorbic Acid (Vitamin C) - Source: synthetic or corn. Use: nutrient. **Kosher, pareve without supervision.**

Ascorbyl Palmitate -Source: synthetic and palm oil. Use: preservative. **Kosher, pareve without supervision.**

Benzoic Acid - Source: synthetic. Use: preservative. **Kosher, pareve without supervision.**

BHA (Butylated hydroxanisole)- Source: synthetic. Use: as an antioxidant in cereals, stabilizers, shortenings, and potato flakes and granules. **Kosher, pareve without supervision when found in corn oil.**

BHT (Butylated hydroxytoluene)- Source: synthetic. Use: as an antioxidant in beverages, desserts, cereals, glazed fruits, dry mixes for beverages, and potato flakes and granules. **Kosher, pareve without supervision when found in corn oil**

Calcium Alginate - see Alginates.

Calcium Carbonate - Source: limestone. Use: tooth powder and in removing acidity of wine. **Kosher, pareve without supervision.**

Calcium Chloride - Source: synthetic. Use: in canned goods and in cottage and cheddar cheeses as a preservative. **Kosher, pareve without supervision.**

Calcium Citrate - See Citric Acid.

Calcium Disodium (EDTA) - Source: synthetic. Use: flavor retention in canned soda and canned white potatoes; as a preservative in dressings, egg products, oleomargarine, potato salad, lima beans, mushrooms, pecan pie filling, and spreads. **Kosher, pareve without supervision.**

Calcium Propionate - Source: synthetic. Use: preservative. **Kosher, supervision preferred.**

Calcium Stearate - Source: a compound of calcium and stearic acid. (**IMPORTANT: see Stearic Acid**) Use: anti-caking ingredient in some spices (especially garlic salt and onion salt) and extensively in tablets. **Requires supervision.**

Calcium Sorbate - Source: synthetic. Use: preservative. **Kosher, pareve without supervision.**

Calcium Stearol Lactylate - Source: milk or soybeans. Use: instant mashed potatoes. **Requires supervision.**

Calcium Stearoyl Lactylate - Source: chemical reaction of stearic acid and lactic acid. Use: as a dough conditioner, whipping agent and as a conditioner in dehydrated potatoes. **Requires supervision.**

Caprylic Acid - Sources: palm oil, coconut oil. Use: preservative and flavoring. **Kosher, pareve without supervision.**

Carbon Black - Source: synthetic. Use: black coloring in confectionery. **Requires supervision.**

Carmine (Cochineal) - Source: insect. A crimson pigment derived from a Mexican species of scale insert (coccus cacti) Use: coloring in red apple sauce, fruit cocktail, confections, baked goods, meats, and spices. **Not kosher.**

Carrageenan - Sources: seaweed and Irish moss. Use: as a substitute for gelatin (an emulsifier, stabilizer, and food thickener). **Kosher, pareve without supervision.**

Caramel - Source: sugar or glucose. Use: coloring foods, beverages, and confectionery items. **Kosher, pareve without supervision.**

Casein - Source: milk, hence dairy. Uses: stabilizer for confectionery, texturizer for ice cream and sherbets, or as a replacement for egg albumin. Because it is precipitated by acid or by animal or vegetable enzymes, **requires supervision.**

Castoreum - Source: Beaver Glands. **Not Kosher.**

Catalase - Source: cow liver. Use: coagulant. **Requires supervision.**

Cholic Acid - Source: animal bile. Use: emulsifier in dried egg whites. **Requires supervision.**

Choline Bitartrate - Source: animal tissue. Use: nutrient (B-complex vitamin). **Requires supervision.**

Citric Acid - Sources: fruits and vegetables, molasses and grain. Use: antioxidant, sugar solubilizing in ice cream and sherbet, fruit juice drinks, and canned and jarred produts, including jelly, cheese, candy, carbonated beverages, instant potatoes, wheat, chips, potato sticks, wine. **Kosher, pareve without supervision.**

Civet, Absolute - Source: cats. Use: flavoring for beverages, ice cream, ices, candy, baked goods and chewing gum. **Not Kosher.**

Cocoa Butter - Source: cocoa bean. Use: chocolate coatings. **Kosher, pareve without supervision.**

Coconut Oil - Source: coconut. Use: in the manufacture of edible fats, chocolate, and candies; in baking in place of lard. **Requires supervision (see Oil).**

Confectionery Glaze - See Resinous Glaze and Shellac.

Corn Starch -Source: Corn. **Kosher parve without supervision.**

Cream of Tartar (Tartaric Acid) - Source: argol, the stony sediment of wine casks. Once the liquid residue has been removed from the argols by aging one year and drying, the argols are permissible. Use: in a variety of confections and in the preparation of baked goods.

Cysteine. L form - Source: an Amino Acid, human and horse, or synthetic (sometimes from deceased women). Use: nutrient in bakery products.

Dextrin - Source: starch. Use: prevents caking of sugar in candy, encapsulates flavor oils in powdered mixes, thickener. **Kosher, pareve without supervision.**

Dextrose (corn syrup) - Source: starch. Use: sweetener, coloring agent in beverages, ice cream, candy and baked goods. **Kosher, pareve without supervision.**

Dilauryl Thiodiproprionate - Source: synthetic. Use: preservative. **Kosher, pareve without supervision.**

Dough Conditioners - Source: calcium stearoyl-2-Lactylate, or animal fat. Use: to improve the texture of bread. Often it will contain mono and diglycerides. **Requires supervision.**

Emulsifiers - Source: fats (animal or vegetable, synthetic.) Use: binding oils and water, thickening, a preservative in baked goods, reducing ice crystals and air bubbles in ice cream. **Requires supervision.**

Erythrobic Acid - Source: synthetic. Use: preservative. **Kosher, pareve without supervision.**

Eschalots (shallot) - Sources: an onion-like plant. Bulbs used like garlic for flavoring. **Kosher, pareve without supervision.**

Ethyl Vanillin - Source: synthetic, bark of spruce tree, or wine alcohol. Use: as a flavor instead of vanilla or to fortify it. **Kosher, requires supervision.**

Fats - Source: animal or vegetable. Substances that are solid at room temperature are fats, those that are liquid at room temperature are oils. **Requires supervision.**

Fatty Acids - Source: animal or vegetable fats. Use: emulsifiers, binders, lubricants. **Requires supervision.**

Filberts - A type of hazelnut, when raw or dry roasted **Kosher, pareve without supervision.**

Glucose - Sources: fruits and other plants such as potatoes and corn (see Dextrose). Use: sweetener, coloring agent. **Kosher, pareve without supervision.**

Glyceride - see Mono- and Diglycerides.

Glycine - Source: gelatin, animal or vegetable oil. Sometimes used in cereals. Also as a flavor enhancer. **Requires supervision.**

Glycerol Monostearate - Glycerol monostearate may be of animal origin. **Requires supervision.**

Glycerine - Sources: beef fat, petroleum, or vegetable. Use: as a solvent or humectant (maintains the desired level of moisture). **Requires supervision.**

Grape Products - see Wine page 197.

Gum Arabic, Gum Acacia - Source: trees. Use: thickening agent, emulsifier, stabilizer. **Kosher, pareve without supervision.**

Gum Base - Sources: trees (chicle, natural rubber, etc.), synthetic butyl rubber, paraffin, polyethylene, vinyl, resin, glycerin, glycerol monostearate. Use: in the manufacture of chewing gums. **Requires supervision.**

Gum Guaiac - Source: trees. Use: antioxidant. **Kosher, pareve without supervision.**

Guar Gum - Source: plants. Use: extender for pectin, stabilizer and thickener for spreads, syrups, sauces, salad dressing and licorice. **Kosher, pareve without supervision.**

Gum Tragacanth - Source: shrubs. Use: thickening agent. Herb derived from green leaves or herbaceous part of the plant. **Kosher, pareve without supervision.**

Invert Sugar (Inversol nulomoline colorose)- Source: cane sugar. Use: sweetener. **Kosher, pareve without supervision.**

Invertase (invertin) - Source: yeast. Use: preparation of invert sugar from sucrose. **Kosher, pareve without supervision.**

Lactalbumin - see Albumin.

Lactic Acid - Sources: molasses, corn starch, glucose, molasses. Use: preservative, flavoring. (Lactic acid can also be produced from whey, in which case it is dairy, but its use is restricted to ice cream and cream cheese.). **Kosher, pareve without supervision.**

Lactose (milk sugar) - Source: whey. Use: sweetener, humectant, and nutrient. **Kosher, dairy without supervision.**

Lauric Fats - Source: coconut, palm oil. Use: with or instead of cocoa butter. **Kosher, pareve without supervision.**

Lecithin - Source: soybeans, corn oil. Use: emulsifier and preservative, especially in chocolate. **Kosher, pareve without supervision.**

Lipids - Source: animal or vegetable fat. Use: shortening, flavoring, thickener. **Requires supervision.**

Lysine, L and DL Forms - Sources: casein, fibrin, blood. Usually synthesized. **Supervision recommended.**

Magnesium Stearate - Source: stearic acid. From tallow, vegetable oils or synthetic. Use: anti-caking agent. **Requires supervision.**

Malt Syrup - Source: malt and barley. Use: emulsifier and starch dissolving. **Kosher, pareve without supervision.**

Mannitol - Source: fungi. Use: sweetener. **Kosher, pareve without supervision.**

Methylparaben - Source: synthetic. Use: preservative. **Kosher, pareve without supervision.**

Methyl P Hydroxy Benzoate - see Methylparaben.

Mono- and Diglycerides - Source: animal and vegetable. Use: stabilizer, emulsifier, softener, preservative. Most are animal products. Mono- and diglycerides do not necessarily have to be listed in the ingredients. **Requires supervision.**

Monosodium Glutamate - Source: sugar, plants, beets and corn. Use: flavor enhancer. **Kosher, pareve without supervision.**

Musk - Source: deer glands, synthetic. Use: in flavorings, for beverages, ice cream, candy, baked goods, and chewing gum. Now usually it is produced synthetically.

Natural Fruit Flavors - Concentrated under vacuum or freeze dried. Concentrated fruit pulp that is used in confectionery usually requires fortification with some synthetic flavor. Can contain grape juice, as well as many other non-kosher substances. **Requires supervision.**

Oil of Lemon - Source: lemon peel. **Kosher, parve, without supervision.**

Oil of Rose - Source: distilled from fresh rose petals. Comes mostly from bulgarian damask rose. **Kosher, parve without supervision.**

Oleic Acid - Source: fats and oils (animal or vegetable). Use: defoaming, flavoring. **Requires supervision.**

Oil of Caraway - Source: seeds of Carum Carui. Grown in Holland and Central and Southern Europe. Flavoring for Chocolate and Coatings. **Kosher, pareve without supervision.**

Oil of Cardamon (grains of paradise) - Source: Alleppy Cardamon, trees from India.. Use: enhance the flavor of ground coffee, butter, chocolate, liquor, spice and vanilla flavoring. **Kosher, parve without supervision.**

Oil of Cassia (Cassia Bark) - Source: leaves and Twigs of the chinese cinnamon - Use: for cocoa flavor in biscuits, cakes, ice cream and beverages. **Kosher, parve without supervision.**

Oil of Celery - Source: celery plant. It comes primarily from France. Use: usually as flavoring for cocoa, chocolate, and other confections. **Kosher, parve without supervision.**

Oil of Cinnamon - Source: under the bark of the Cinnamonum Zeylanicum tree. Found in Seychelles and Ceylon. Use: to enhance fruit flavorings. **Kosher, parve without supervision.**

Oil of Peppermint - Source: dried plant leaves. Use: flavoring. **Kosher, pareve without supervision.**

Oxysterins - Source: Glycerides, stearic acid. Use: prevents oil from clouding. **Requires supervision.**

Ox Bile - Source: ox bile. Use: preservative and emulsifier in dried egg whites. **Requires supervision.**

Ox Gall - see Ox Bile.

Peanut Oil - Source: oil prepared from peanuts. **Kosher, requires supervision.**

Pectin - Source: roots, stems and fruits of plants. Use: to thicken jellies. **Kosher, pareve without supervision.**

Pepper Cream - Source: herb. Use: spice. Requires di-glycerides or other emulsifiers to mix. **Kosher, pareve, requires supervision.**

Pepsin - Source: enzyme, usually extracted from hog stomachs, but can be synthetic. Use: coagulant in cheese. Can be produced from kosher animals. **Requires supervision.**

Polyglycerol Esters of Fatty Acids - Source: fats and oils, animal or vegetable. **Requires supervision.**

Polysorbate 60, 65, 80 - Source: stearic acid (also called Tween). Use: emulsifiers, especially in "non-dairy" products. **Require supervision.**

Potassium Bi sulfite - Source: synthetic. Use: preservative. **Kosher, pareve without supervision.**

Potassium Caseinate - Source: milk. Use: stabilizer and texturizer. **Requires supervision.**

Potassium Metabisulfite - Source: synthetic. Use: preservative. **Kosher, pareve without supervision.**

Potassium Sorbate - Source: berries or synthetic. Use: preservative. **Kosher, pareve without supervision.**

Propionic Acid - Source: synthetic or may be made from cheese. Use: mold inhibitor, preservative. **Kosher, requires supervision.**

Propyl Gallate - Source: synthetic or from nuts produced by insects. Use: preservative.

Propylene Glycol (Alginate) - Source: synthetic. Use: emulsifier, stabilizer, solvent. **Kosher, pareve without supervision.**

Propylparaben - Source: synthetic. Use: preservative, **Kosher, pareve without supervision.**

Release Agents - Source: oils, mineral oil, mono-glycerides or synthetic. Use: keeps heated foods from sticking to equipment, utensils, and packaging. These need not be listed in the ingredients. **Requires supervision.**

Resinous Glaze - Source: insect secretion. Use: coating candies and pills. While there are authorities who permit these glazes on the grounds that they are non-edible, there are other authorities who forbid them.

Rennet - Source: animal enzymes. Derived from the lining membrane of the stomach of suckling calves. Use: coagulant and curdling agent especially in cheese and other dairy products. A vegetable enzyme similar to rennet is available as a substitute, but even if it is used, supervision is required. Hard cheese made by gentiles without constant supervision, even if made with completely kosher ingredients, is not kosher. (see cheese article) **Requires supervision.**

Rennin - see Rennet.

Serum Albumin - Source: blood. See Albumin. **Not Kosher.**

Shellac - Source: insect secretion. Use: in glaze for confectionery products and in chocolate panning. See Resinous Glazes.

Shortenings - Source: oil. Use: to make baked goods light and flaky. Factories often make both animal and vegetable shortenings on the same equipment. **Requires supervision.**

Sodium Alginate - Source: seaweed or kelp. Use: as a stabilizer. **Kosher, pareve without supervision.**

Sodium Ascorbate - Source: synthetic. Use: preservative. **Kosher, pareve without supervision.**

Sodium Benzoate - Source: synthetic origin. Use: preservative. **Kosher, pareve without supervision.**

Sodium Bisulfite - Source: synthetic. Use: preservative. **Kosher, pareve without supervision.**

Sodium Caseinate - Source: milk and cheese. Use: texturizer in "nondairy" creamers and instant mashed potatoes. **Kosher, dairy – requires supervision.**

Sodium Citrate - Source: synthetic. Use: emulsifier and buffer in processed produce. **Kosher, pareve without supervision.**

Sodium Lauryl Sulfate - Source: synthetic. Use: detergent, whipping agent, an emulsifier (in egg products) and surfactant (in beverages). **Kosher, pareve without supervision.**

Sodium Meta Bisulfate - Source: synthetic. Use: preservative. **Kosher, pareve without supervision.**

Sodium Propionate - Source: synthetic origin or rarely it is made from cheese. Use: mold preventative. **Kosher, supervision preferred.**

Sodium Nitrite - Source: synthetic. Use: preservative. **Kosher, pareve without supervision.**

Sodium Sorbate - Source: synthetic or from corn. Use: preservative. **Kosher, pareve without supervision.**

Sodium Sulfite - Source: synthetic. Use: preservative. **Kosher, pareve without supervision.**

Softeners - Sources: animal or vegetable. Use: in chewing gum. **Requires supervision.**

Sorbic Acid - Sources: berries, corn or synthetic. Use: mold inhibitor. **Kosher, pareve without supervision.**

Sorbitan Monostearate - Source: Stearic acid. Use: emulsifier, defoamer, flavor disperser. **Requires supervision.**

Span - see Polysorbate.

Spearmint Oil - Source: the herb mentha viriais. Use: primarily as flavoring in chewing gum. **Kosher, pareve without supervision.**

Sperm oil - Source: whale. Use: release agent and lubricant in baking pans. **Not kosher.**

Spices - Source: dried vegetable product derived from any part of the plant, whether root, stem, bark, fruit, bud or seed. **Kosher, without supervision**

Stannous Chloride - Source:synthetic. Use: preservative. **Kosher, pareve without supervision.**

Stearic Acid - Source: animal or vegetable oil. Use: in butter and vanilla flavoring, Softener in chewing gum. **Requires supervision.**

Stearyl Lactylic Acid - Source: fats and oils. Use: emulsifier. **Requires supervision.** (Kosher forms are often dairy.)

Sulfur Dioxide - Source: synthetic gas Use: preservative. **Kosher, pareve without supervision.**

Tartaric Acid - see Cream of Tartar.

Thiodipropionic Acid - Source:synthetic. Use: preservative, or from cheese. **Kosher, requires supervision.**

Tocopherols - Source: synthetic, or soybeans. Use: preservative, nutrient (Vitamin E). **Kosher pareve without supervision.**

Tragacanth - see Gum Tragacanth.

Tricalcium Phosphate - Source: synthetic. Use: anti-caking agent, bleaching agent. **Kosher, pareve without supervision.**

Turmeric - Source: herb. Use: spice. As a powder: (Often used in its oleo resin form for use in pickling brine and mustard with glycearides added.) **kosher, requires supervision.**

Tween and Span - see Polysorbate.

Vanilla - Source: bean. Use: flavoring, it may be processed with glycerine. **Requires supervision.**

Vanillin - Source: bark of spruce tree. Use: flavoring. **Kosher, pareve without supervision.**

Vegetable Oil - see Oil.

Vegetable Shortening - see Shortening.

Vegetable Gums - Use: substitute for gelatin in desserts and candies. **Kosher, pareve without supervision.** Also see gum.

Whey - Source: milk, hence dairy. Use: Binder and flavoring agent. Since it is obtained in the manufacture of cheese. **Requires supervision.**

FLAVORINGS

The F.D.A. definition of flavors is as follows:

Natural flavor (or natural flavoring) is the essential oil, oleonesic, essence or extractive, protein hydrolysate, distillate or any product of roasting, heating or enzymolysis which contains the flavoring constituents derived from a spice, fruit or fruit juice, vegetable or vegetable juice, edible yeast, herb, bark, bud, root, leaf, or similar plant material, meat, seafood, poultry, eggs, dairy products, or fermentation products thereof, whose significant function in food is flavoring rather than nutritional.

Artificial flavor (or artificial flavoring) is any substance, the function of which is to impart flavor which is not derived from the sources indicated above.

This definition makes it obvious that the kosher consumer is faced with the two ubiquitous kashrus problems concerning flavorings: source and process.

"Natural" flavor by the above definition includes derivatives of meat, seafood, poultry, eggs, dairy products, or fermentation products. Every one of these "natural" flavor sources requires supervision. The derivative flavor, therefore, also requires supervision. The definition allows afrold (from the sassafras root) to be called "natural," although, in fact, it has been banned by the F.D.A (1960) as a cause of liver cancer. Coumarin, a liver poison banned in 1954, qualifies as "natural." We are now even told there is such a thing as "natural" margarine (derived from polyester cow's milk?)!

If this label "natural" were not confusing enough, it is possible for pure fresh-squeezed lime juice to be labeled "artificial flavor" (if it is used to enhance the flavor of a lemon product). Consequently, "artificial flavor" does not mean "laboratory produced."

Unfortunately for the kosher consumer, the F.D.A. labeling requirements do not coincide with Jewish law. Labels cannot be relied upon for kashrus information.

Of the processes mentioned in the F.D.A. definition- hydrolysis, distillation, roasting, heating, enzymolysis, and fermentation- the last four can conceivably be the sources of kashrus problems. Peanuts, for example, may be "roasted" in oil. Heating may be done with equipment and utensils which have been used for non-kosher processing. The enzymes for enzymolysis can be derived from microorganisms of plants or animals. Therefore, the processes, too, must be under supervision.

A list of commonly used natural flavorings reveals many items which are inherently not kosher:

AMBERGRIS - Source: sperm whale intestines. Use: berry, fruit, rum, spice, and vanilla flavoring for beverages, ice cream, ices, candy, and baked goods. **Not Kosher.**

CIVET, ABSOLUTE - Source: secretion from receptacle between the anus and genitals of cats. Use: raspberry, butter, caramel, grape, and rum flavorings in beverages, ice cream, ices, candy, baked good, gelatin desserts, and chewing gum. **Not Kosher.**

CASTOREUM - Beaver glands extract used as a flavoring. **Not Kosher.**

COGNAC OIL (Wine Yeast Oil) obtained from the distillation of wine -Use: berry, cherry, grape, brandy, and rum flavorings for beverages, ice cream, ices, candy, baked goods, gelatin desserts, condiments, and liquors. **Requires supervision.**

MUSK - Source: deer glands. Use: fruit, cherry, maple, mint, nut, black walnut, pecan, spice, vanilla, molasses flavorings in beverages, ice cream, ices, candy, baked goods, gelatin desserts, pudding, chewing gum, and syrups. **Not Kosher.**

OLEIC ACID - Source: animal or vegetable fats and oils. Use: butter, cheese, ice cream, ices, candy, baked goods, condiments, and spice flavorings in beverages. **Requires supervision.**

One rather common ingredient used in flavorings can be derived from cream. The product in which it appears synthesized through fermentation would then be classified as dairy.

ACETOIN (Acetyl Methyl Carbinol). Sources: fermentation of cream. Use: flavoring agent in raspberry, strawberry, butter, butterscotch, caramel, coconut, coffee, fruit, liquor, rum, nut, walnut, vanilla, cream soda, cheese flavorings for beverages, ice cream, ices, candy, baked goods, margarine, gelatin desserts, cottage cheese, and shortenings. May be dairy. **Requires supervision.**

Following is a clear example of how one can be misled by relying on the label of product containing natural or artifical food flavoring.

FOOD FLAVOR

Natural Flavor (or natural flavoring) – the essential oil, oleoresin, essence or extractive, protein hydrolysate, distillate or any product of roasting, heating or enzymolysis which contains the flavoring constituents derived from a spice, fruit or fruit juice, vegetable or vegetable juice, edible yeast, herb, bark, bud, root, leaf, or similar plant material, meat, seafood, poultry, eggs, dairy products, or fermentation products thereof, whose significant function in food is flavoring rather than nutritional.

Artificial Flavor (or artificial flavoring) – any substance, the function of which is to impart flavor which is not derived from the sources indicated above.

F.D.A. definition

Suppose, though, that there were not enough plums to flavor the product by themselves, or that a food processor wanted to enhance the flavor – and why not? Plums vary in sweetness and flavor, and if you, the customer, are familiar with a product and like it, you will want it to be the same each and every time you buy it; therefore additional flavor might be added. The flavor would be either natural, stemming from plums themselves, or artificial. If natural flavor is added, the label would read, "Plum Flavored Pudding" or "Natural Plum Flavored Pudding." Notice in the latter that the words *natural* and *flavored* are both used. **Those are the key words.** There is flavor added, and it is natural flavor.

Now then, if natural flavor other than plum is present, the label would read, "Plum Flavored Pudding, with Other Natural Flavor." Note that specific reference is made to "other natural flavor". You can be sure it is a natural flavor, but one other than plum flavor.

Flavoring	Food Name
Vanilla Extract	Vanilla Pudding
Vanilla Extract and other natural flavor(s)	
	Vanilla Pudding, with other Natural Flavor

Natural flavoring other than vanilla, or any artificial vanilla flavor (presence of *any* artificial flavor that simulates the flavor indicated on the carton automatically requires designation as "artificial")

> Artificially Flavored Vanilla Pudding or
> Vanilla Pudding, Artificially Flavored

When characterizing ingredients are expected, it will read as follows:

Plums (enough to characterize the food)

> Plum Pudding

Plums (not enough to characterize the food independently) and

(1) Natural plum flavor   Plum Flavored Pudding, or Natural Plum Flavored Pudding

(2) Natural flavors other than plum

> Plum Flavored Pudding, with Other Natural Flavor or Natural Plum Flavored Pudding, with Other Natural Flavor

GENERAL PRODUCTS LIST
(FOR YEAR ROUND USE ONLY)

ALUMINUM FOIL - Requires no supervision.

BABY FOOD - **Requires supervision** for all forms: vegetables, fruits, cereals, and puddings. Common problems: equipment used for non-kosher products, mono- and di-glycerides added, non-kosher flavoring.

BAGELS - (See Bread, page 157.)

BAKERIES and BREADS - (See separate article, page 157.)

BEVERAGES - **Requires supervision in many cases.** Common problems: grape products, flavorings, colorings, stabilizers. It is important to note that many soft drinks need not list all their ingredients by name on the label. (See beverage article page 158.)

BLINTZES, EGG ROLLS - **Requires supervision.** Common problems: oil, eggs, cheese, equipment and utensils used for other, non-kosher foods.

BREAD - **Requires supervision.** Common problem: oil, mono- and di-glycerides, shortening, release agents. (See page 157.)

BUTTER - All grade AA and grade AAA butters are kosher (dairy) without supervision.

CANDIES - (See separate article, page 159.)

CAKES, CAKE MIXES, DOUGHNUTS, PASTRIES AND PIES - **All require supervision** and can be assumed to be non-kosher without certification. Common problems: di-glycerides, shortenings (lard is extremely common because of its unique flaking quality and its high absorbency).

146

The fillings and creams may contain fats, emulsifiers, and stabilizers. Also, be careful to check for dairy ingredients.

CANNED FRUITS AND VEGETABLES - It has been generally accepted that commonly used canned (including jarred) fruits and vegetables do not present a kashrus problem. Peas, carrots, string beans, sweet potatoes, asparagus, beets, peaches, pears, etc., are usually processed seasonally by canneries in plants producing only fruits and vegetables. Recently, however, some companies that process dry pack vegetables have manufactured canned (including bottled) vegetables on the same processing equipment as non-kosher meat products. This situation has long existed with canned tomato juice, vegetable juice, prepared sauces, chow mein vegetables, canned soups and baked beans. These items are occasionally processed in plants producing similar varieties of products that contain meat or other non-kosher foods. Therefore, these products and any items in which they appear as ingredients may **require supervision**. Reading the label in such a case is not enough! However, in plants that do not produce dry pack vegetables, there is no reason to be concerned in regard to peas, carrots, green beans, corn, etc. In fruit packs, care must be taken that grape juice should not be in the ingredients.

CHEWING GUM: (See article and listing, page 164.)

CHAMPAGNE - See Wine.

CHEESE - All varieties **require supervision** (including rennetless cheese.) (See article, page 161.)

CHOCOLATE: **Requires supervision.** Standards for milk chocolate vary from country to country, and care is necessary. Common problems: whey, emulsifiers, flavors, oils and resinous glazes. The same equipment is often used for milk chocolate and other non-kosher products.

CLEANSERS (Household)- **Requires supervision.** The detergents can be animal derivatives or synthetic.

COFFEE - 100% regular coffee **requires no supervision.**

COFFEES - FLAVORED - Require supervision. Common problems: often they are flavored with non-kosher artificial flavor. They may contain oil as well.

COOKIES AND CRACKERS - Require supervision. Common problems: shortening, oil, flavors, emulsifiers, stabilizers, antioxidants.

Many cookies contain dairy ingredients. However, careful reading of the label is not enough since some plants also produce cookies and crackers on dairy equipment and yet do not indicate this on the label.

COTTAGE CHEESE: (See article and cheese list, page 161.) **Requires supervision.**

DAIRY PRODUCTS - (See article, page 167.)

DISHWASHING DETERGENTS: (See Cleansers.)

DOUGHNUTS: Requires supervision. (See Cake.)

DRESSINGS (Salad): Common problems: Flavoring, stabilizers, gelatin, oil, mono- and di-glycerides. **Requires supervision.**

EGGS - (See article on eggs, page 111.)

EGG SUBSTITUTES: Requires supervision. Common problems: oil, emulsifiers, artificial flavor. (See article, page 113.)

HORSERADISH - Requires supervision. Common problems: vinegar, turmeric, artificial flavor.

INFANT FORMULA - Requires supervision. These products are often either dairy or soy derivatives. Common problem: oil, flavoring, stabilizers & emulsifiers.

ICE CREAM, SHERBET, ICES - Requires supervision. Common problems: flavoring, mono- and diglyceride, stabilizers, emulsifiers, gelatin, whey and oil. (See article, page 189.)

JELLIES, JAMS, AND PRESERVES - Requires supervision. Common problems: gelatin, coloring, flavors, grape products (especially in dark-colored jellies) In Israeli products, the problems include *Ma'aser, Terumah and Shmittah.*

KETCHUP, MUSTARD, VINEGAR - Requires supervision. All three are made with vinegar which may include wine vinegar. Ketchup presents a problem common to tomato products – the possible contamination from utensils and equipment. Mustard is sometimes flavored with oleoresins of turmeric or pepper. Supervision is then required because of the di-glycerides or emulsifiers.

LAUNDRY DETERGENTS - Does not require supervision.

MACARONI - Check for milk and kosher eggs.

MARGARINE - Requires supervision. Common problems: oil, preservatives, flavoring and coloring. (See Margarine article page 190.)

MARSHMALLOWS - (See article page 192.)

MATZAH - See Bread.

MAYONNAISE - Requires supervision. Common problems: oil, vinegar, emulsifiers, eggs, oxystearin, and spices.

MELBA TOAST - See Bread. **Requires supervision.**

MUFFINS - See Bread. **Require supervision.**

MUSTARD - See Ketchup. **Requires supervision.**

"NON-DAIRY" PRODUCTS - Used in whipped cream, pareve ice cream, coffee whitener, pareve sour cream, pareve cheese) **Require supervision.** Government standards for "non-dairy" and Jewish law's standards for pareve are very different. Most foods labeled "non-dairy" are not in fact pareve. Some "non-dairy" products are not even kosher. Common problems: whey, calcium caseinate, sodium caseinate, lactalbumin, calcium stearoyl-2-lactylate, lactose (all the above are dairy by common agreement of most rabbinic authorities) polysorbates, oil, and sorbitan monostearate.

Whipped toppings require supervision. Whipped cream often contains stabilizers, mono- and di-glycerides, polysorbates, and oils.

NOODLES - See Pasta.

NUTS - Nuts roasted in oil require supervision even when roasted in "pure vegetable oil". Dry-roasted nuts are ordinarily kosher without supervision. (Caution: some companies add gelatin to their nuts.)

OLIVES - See Canned Fruits and Vegetables. Olives from Israel require reliable supervision. Problem: Teruma, *Maaser, shmitta.* Olives outside Israel which contain **only** olives, water, ascorbic acid, salt and ferrous gluconate do **not** require supervision.

PANCAKE MIXES - **Require supervision.** Problems: emulsifiers, stabilizers, oil, mono- and di-glycerides and flavoring.

PASTA - (Noodles) **Requires supervision.** Common problem: eggs, milk, protein fortifiers, stearates.

PASTRIES - (See Bakery article page 157.)

PEANUT BUTTER - PROCESSED - **Requires supervision.** The common problems are oil and mono- and di-glycerides. "Old Fashioned" peanut butters which list only peanuts and salt as ingredients do not require supervision. Peanut butter with oil added requires supervision. (Even if it is "pure vegetable oil.")

PICKLES - **Require supervision. Common** problem: turmeric, flavoring, non-kosher equipment. Note: government standards regarding the term "kosher pickle" merely require that they contain garlic, and then they are permitted by law to be called "kosher pickle"

PIE - See Cakes.

PITA - See Bread.

PIZZA - **Requires supervision.** Common problem: cheese (see article page 147) oil, flavorings, toppings.

PLASTIC BAGS - **Does not require Supervision.**

PLASTIC WRAP - **Does not require Supervision.**

POLISH, SILVER - **Does not require Supervision.**

POPCORN - Raw popcorn kernels do not require supervision. Microwave popcorn or popcorn kernels prepared in oil **require supervision.** Bagged popcorn and all popcorn sold commercially (theaters, parks, etc.) always require reliable supervision even if one sees they are currently using kosher oil. This is due to the fact that without supervision we have no control or knowledge as to what types of oils have been used in the machinery previously.

POTATO CHIPS - **Requires supervision.** Common problems: oil, spices, equipment and utensils used for production of dairy cheese snacks or non-kosher products.

POTATOES (instant, mashed, hash browns, french fries, etc.)- **Require supervision.** Common problems: oil, emulsifiers, flavoring, mono- and di-glycerides.

POWDERED MILK - See Dairy Products.

PRESERVES - See Jellies.

PRETZELS - See Potato Chips. **Requires supervision.**

PUDDING - **Requires supervision.** Common problems: flavoring, oils, whey, emulsifiers, stabilizers.

RAISINS - **Does not require supervision** when oil is not listed.

RELISH - **Requires supervision.** Common problems: Vinegar, equipment.

RICE - UNSEASONED - **Does not require supervision**

ROLLS - See Bread.

SANDWICH BAGS - **Does not require supervision.**

SAUCES - **Require supervision.** Common problems: oil, wine meat, tomato products, polysorbates, and use of same utensils and equipment for non-kosher products. Worcestershire sauce and steak sauces usually contain fish derivatives causing an additional problem since many authorities forbid the eating of fish and meat at the same time.

SHERBET - See Ice Cream.

SHERRY - (See Wine, page 197.)

SNACKS - (See separate article page 194.)

SOAP - See Cleansers.

SOUPS - **Require supervision.** Common problems: meat, chicken, stabilizers, emulsifiers, and use of the same equipment to produce non-kosher or dairy items.

SPAGHETTI - (See Pasta) Common problems: milk protein fortifiers.

SPICES AND SEASONINGS - Pure spices generally **do not require supervision.** Garlic salt and onion salt require supervision because calcium stearate is often used to prevent lumping. All spices should be checked for calcium stearate. Seasoning usually contain many ingredients some of which require supervision or are not kosher altogether, such as shrimp, etc.

SUGAR - Does not require supervision.

TEHINA MIX - Requires supervision. Common problems: oil, bugs.

VERMOUTH - is wine. **Requires supervision.**

VINEGAR - Does not requires supervision. (Wine vinegar requires supervision.)

VITAMINS - (See separate article, page 194.)

WAX PAPER - Requires supervision.

WINE, LIQUEUR, PREPARED MIXES - Does not require supervision. (See separate listing, page 197.) **Wine yeast requires supervision.**

YEAST - Requires supervision.

YOGURT - Requires supervision. See Dairy Products. Common problems: rennet, gelatin, emulsifiers & stabilizers, flavoring.

PRODUCTS THAT DO NOT REQUIRE CERTIFICATION

Aluminum Foil

Baking Powder

Cocoa - plain, with no additives.

Coffee - Plain - without flavoring.

Corn Starch

Dried Fruit - with no oil or other ingredients listed (except for the usual preservatives, such as potassium sorbate, sulphur dioxide and sodium bisulfate).

Flour - plain only.

Fruits - most plain canned and frozen fruits with no added ingredients besides water, salt, sugar, corn syrup, corn sweetener, citric acid, ascorbic acid, are acceptable without certification. Calcium chloride, lactic acid, and ferrous glutomate do not require certification, but beware of added ingredients such as spices, flavorings, colorings, or grape juice. Grape juice is especially common lately in "juice pack" and diet pack varieties of fruit which contain no added sugar or flavoring.

Gin

Guar Gum

Honey

Molasses

Maraschino Cherries - without added flavoring.

Nuts - plain, with no oil or other ingredients (besides salt) on the label, when they have been dry roasted.

Oats

Pectin

Petroleum

Plastic Bags

Plastic Wraps

Popcorn Kernels - plain, with no oil, flavoring, etc.

Raisins - plain, with no oil listed on the label.

Raw Nuts

Rice - plain, with no flavor or seasoning added.

Riboflavin

Rock Candy - unflavored only.

Rum

Rye - straight liquor.

Saccharin

Sake - pure.

Salt

Sorbitol

Soy Beans

Spices - pure.

Starch

Sugar

Tequila -without worm. (See article, page 200.)

Tea - plain, with no added ingredients or flavorings.

Vegetables - fresh and frozen - pure. Care must be taken to check for worms in leafy vegetables. (see page 222.)

Wheat

Wheat Germ - with no added ingredients.

SOME PRODUCTS & INGREDIENTS
REQUIRING KOSHER CERTIFICATION

Albumen

Argol

Calcium Stearate

Calcium Stearoyl-2-Lactylate

Caviar

Chocolate

Cognac Oil

Di-glycerides

Dough Conditioners

Emulsifiers

Fatty Acids

Filled Candies

Filleted Fish

Flavorings

Food Colorings

Glycerine

Glyceride

Glycerol

Glycerol Monostearate

Glycine

Jellies and Jams

Shortening

Softeners

Sorbitan Monostearate

Stabilizers

Stearates

Stearic Acid

Turmeric (as an ingredient) when it is liquid based.

Tuna Fish

Tween

Vanilla

Vegetable Oil

Whey

BAKERIES

Bakeries require supervision, even if the ingredient list seems acceptable, or the bakery bakes "Jewish Bread" or "challah." Common problems include: shortening, emulsifiers, equipment and utensils, and use of dairy ingredients. Bakeries without supervision use the same equipment for baking their non-kosher products and their "Jewish products." Hence all the products are non-kosher. Even kosher bakeries frequently use the same utensils for their dairy products and their pareve products. Hence, all the products, even the "pareve" items, would really be dairy.

(The use of dairy ingredients in bread is forbidden by the *Shulchan Aruch,* chapter 97.)

In addition, breads from a bakery owned by Jews requires the "taking of challah," which may not have been performed at the bakery. The mitzvah can be fulfilled at home by placing all bakery goods in one room, opening all the packages, and removing and burning a small piece from one of the loaves. If some of the loaves are from different kinds of flour (for example, wheat and rye), challah must be taken from a loaf of each type.

BREAD - (including bagels, breadsticks, matzah, melba toast, muffins, pita, and rolls) - **REQUIRE SUPERVISION.** Common problems: shortening, oil, dough mixes, dough conditioners (made from shortening and di-glycerides). Release agents (to grease the pan, and these need not be listed on the label!), dairy textures, eggs, egg substitutes, and equipment and utensils used for a variety of products. Dough mixes can contain shortening and oils that require supervision.

BEVERAGES

T he vast array of drinks available to the consumer today is sometimes overwhelming. The gamut runs from pure water, extra pure water, imported extra pure water, etc. all the way to beverages with over 20 ingredients. Some of the problems that the kosher consumer must be aware of concerning drinks are: flavoring, oil, glycerol, glycerine, gelatin, grape juice, processing on non-kosher equipment

Sodas consist primarily of water and sugar. Colas for instance have up to 8 teaspoons full of sugar per can. The major thing that differentiates each soda is the flavoring. Unfortunately, the F.D.A. allows the bottling companies to put many flavors together under the title "artificial flavors." Even if the label reads "natural flavors," this can include grape juice, because grape juice is indeed a "natural flavor." Also, orange soda often contains brominated vegetable oil, which acts as an emulsifier and gives the soda a thicker look, making it appear more palatable to the consumer. Although pure orange juice is truly pure, orange drink or fruit punch can contain many non-kosher additives. Most sodas today have some type of certification. Care must be taken to always make sure that the supervision extends to the local bottling plants. Welch's grape soda for instance has the reliable supervision of the O/K Laboratories. This certification, however, only covers part of the East coast, and has no relevance to the Welch's soda sold elsewhere in the U.S.. Tomato juice occasionally is processed on the same equipment as clam juice, etc. and therefore requires reliable supervision.

Sodas may contain non-kosher glycerine, flavorings, and other problem ingredients. Although soda labels list fewer than 10 ingredients, there may be 4 times as many different ingredients in such products. In addition, imitation grape, black cherry, and punch-flavored sodas may contain non-kosher wine or grape juice. An additional problem is the use of castorium (derived from beaver sex glands) in some berry-flavored drinks. Therefore, sodas and other drink mixes should not be used unless kosher approved. This also applies to fruit-flavored drinks, whether canned, frozen or fresh, for non-kosher stabilizers may also be used.

CANDIES

T here was once a time when the kashrus status of candy was very simple and could be determined very quickly. All one had to do was ask the person who made it in their home, usually one's grandmother. After investigating this close-to-home source, they most probably would find that it was made by melting cane sugar together with some berry or other natural fruit flavor. In those days life was simple. Today, we are faced with a candy industry that is the ninth largest food producer in the U.S. Instead of producing a limited number of old fashioned candy varieties, over 1,200 modern-day candy companies produce nearly 2,000 varieties of confections. Considering the fact that to produce this much candy, over 73 million pounds of eggs and an incredible array of flavorings are used, it behooves the kosher consumer to learn the facts about the candies on the market today.

Some of the Problems

In order to extend the shelf life of candies, ingredients such as hydrogenated shortenings, emulsifiers and anti-oxidants are added, which commonly include mono- and di-glycerides (sometimes processed from animal fat), propylene glycol, egg yolk (sometimes ova—unlaid eggs from non-kosher chickens) and gelatin. Some specific problems with candies are:

Marshmallows:
Gelatin (there is very little gelatin made from kosher slaughtered animals available anywhere in the world today).

Hard Candies:
Oils, flavorings (can be a grape derivative, among other problems).

Creme Candies:
Glycerin (to retain moisture).

Chocolates:
Monostearate (often animal de-

rivative, used as a bloom inhibitor) emulsifiers, shortenings, oil.

Jelly Candy:

Flavorings, gelatin, anti-oxidants

Whipped Candies, Nougats, Frappes:

Albumen (sometimes from non-kosher eggs); gelatin.

In conclusion, while we have greatly benefited over the years from many additional types of candies, we are likewise faced with many additional problems in eating them. However, with so many companies vying for a larger share of the market, many companies have sought and obtained reliable kosher certification for their products.

CHEESE

I n an age where a substance intended for use as butter is in reality made of whale oil and one intended to substitute for egg whites is made from chemically treated animal blood, it is refreshing to know that there is still one entire family of foods being manufactured today by a method which has remained virtually un-changed for centuries. This genre of edibles is renowned for its nutritional and gastro-nomic virtues, and all connoisseurs of good food have their favorites among its varied types: cheeses.

These all-natural delectables are not, however, without their halachic problems, as we shall see. The kosher consumer should not be led to assume that natural, old-fashioned foods are necessarily kosher. After all, even whale oil is quite natural and old-fashioned.

All of the many varieties of commercially prepared cheeses avail-able to today's consumer are produced by the same basic process, an ancient and efficient one. A type of bacteria, known in the cheese trade as a "starter," is added to a quantity of milk, souring the milk. In chemist's terms, the lactose in the milk turns to lactic acid. Next, a curdling agent is added, and this coagulates part of the milk coming out a watery liquid known as whey. Whereas this mixture may be sufficiently processed for the likes of Miss Muffet, cheese afficionados prefer the results which come when the whey is drawn off and the curds are treated in a variety of fashions, resulting in a variety of cheeses.

The second step in the above process, the addition of the curdling agent, is where the kashrus question arises.

The most common curdling agent, known as rennet, generally comes from animal sources, specifically the lining of the stomachs of calves. Such an exotic ingredient is necessary because the enzymes therein are the only chemicals known to efficiently and effectively curdle milk. It seems that long ago, people realized this fact when they saw recently suckled milk curdling in the stomach of a just slaughtered calf and they experimented with scrapings of the stomach lining.

Anthropology aside, the fact that there are kashrus implications in the use of rennet is obvious.

If the source of rennet is a kosher species of animal, ritually slaughtered under rabbinical supervision, it may be used to turn milk into cheese. For rather involved halachic reasons, there is no problem of meat and milk mixing in such usage. Likewise, if rennet is extracted, as it occasionally is, from vegetable sources, there is no question as to the kashrus of the cheese when it is produced under rabbinical supervision.

However, most commercial cheeses (except those produced under rabbinical supervision) are made with rennet derived from animals slaughtered by conventional non-kosher means.

Even though there is a kashrus principle which generally allows minuscule quantitites of non-kosher ingredients to be, at least after the fact, legally overwhelmed by great quantities of kosher ingredients and rendered nonexistent, this principle cannot, unfortunately, be applied in the case of rennet. This is because rennet has an unmistakable coagulant effect on milk; where one substance visibly solidifies another, the solidifying agent is always considered a substantial factor, whatever its amount.

An additional factor in prohibiting standard commercial cheeses, even when produced by using microbial agents for curdling as a substitute for rennet, is the existence of an ancient decree banning the use of cheeses produced by non-Jews.

It would seem, up to this point, that the wonderful world of cheese would have to be added to the other delights which observant Jews forego to meet G-d's standards for them.

But, where there's a will, of course, there's a "whey."

As a response to the kashrus problems of cheese-making, several kosher cheese companies make use of rennet derived from exclusively kosher sources. Cheeses produced in this way are of the same quality and boast the same variety as their non-kosher counterparts. There is a good reason for this: the kosher cheese market at present cannot support the considerable outlay of capital required to purchase both the cheese-producing machinery and the expertise of giant non-kosher cheese companies. Therefore, special kosher runs are done at the standard cheese companies. A kashrus supervisor kashers any equipment requiring it, and sees to it that the next run of cheeses is produced using only kosher rennet. The rest is done by routine techniques, under rabbinical supervision, which gives the cheese the status of "Jewish-produced."

Observant cheese lovers are therefore not deprived of their high-quality delicacy. The rental of time and machinery and the cost of reliable supervision makes kosher cheese a bit more expensive than non-kosher, but the deal is certainly a bargain!

NOTE: The general prohibition against all cheeses made by gentiles without supervision includes RENNETLESS CHEESE.

Therefore cheese requires supervision in all forms, including hard cheeses (such as American, Cheddar, Muenster, Swiss, etc.) and soft cheese (such as cottage, cream, farmer, and pot cheese).

CHEWING GUM

In 1939, when the Federal Food, Drug, and Cosmetic Act was passed, chewing gum was classified as a food– and rightly so. Approximaely two-thirds of a stick of gum is swallowed and enters the digestive tract. Chewing gum manufacturers managed to secure an exemption from the labeling requirements for foods because it is impractical to list 25 ingredients on a package as small as the one that gum comes in. As many as 15 natural and synthetic ingredients are lumped together as gum base. Soon after 1939, another dozen or so ingredients were allowed to be designated softeners, and the F.D.A. itself suggested the reduction in the labeling of the sweeteners in gum. Incredibly, the F.D.A. also allowed gum manufacturers to not list sugar (60 percent of the average stick of gum) in the first position in the ingredient list, a common requirement for most products.

Consequently, the typical gum wrapper ingredient listing reads: "Made of gum base, sugar, corn syrups, flavor, and softeners." Only two of the more than 40 ingredients are recognizable. Some of the ingredients that do not appear on the label are: chicquilul, crown gum, masaranduba chocolate, residinha, ehilte, glycerin ester of partially hydrogenated wood resin, sodium stearate, potassium stearate, sodium sulphate, sodium sulfide. The two stearate ingredients are of special kashrus concern: stearates usually are animal derivatives.

The kosher consumer cannot tell what ingredients go into the gum from the wrapper, and therefore the only reliable rule is to avoid gums that are not known to be kosher.

THE FOLLOWING IS THE FDA REQUIREMENTS FOR GUM:

MASTICATORY SUBSTANCES
NATURAL (COAGULATED OR CONCENTRATED LATICES) OF VEGETABLE ORIGIN

FAMILY	GENUS AND SPECIES
Sapotaceae:	
Chicle	Manilkara zapotilla Gilly and Manikara chicle Gitty.
Chiquibul	Manilkara zapotilla Gilly.
Crown gum	Manilkara zapotilla Gilly and Manikara chicle Gilly.
Gutta hang kang	Palaquium leiocarpum Boerl, and Palaquium oblongifolium Burck.

MASTICATORY SUBSTANCES (Continued)
NATURAL (COAGULATED OR CONCENTRATED LATICES) OF VEGETABLE ORIGIN

FAMILY

GENUS AND SPECIES

Massaranduba balata (and the
solvent-free resin extract of
Massaranduba balata). .... Manilkara huberi (Ducke) Chevalier.

Sapotaceae–Continued

Massaranduba chocolate .... Manilkara solimoesensis gilly.

Nispero.. Manilkara zapotilla Gilly and Manilkara chicle gilly.

Rosidinha (rosadinha)............................ Micropholis (also known as Sideroxylon) spp.

Venezuelan chicle .... Manilkara williamsii Standley and related spp.

Apocynaceae:

Jetulong... Dyera costulata Hook, F. and Dyera lowii Hook, F.

Leche caspi (sorva) .... Couma macrocarpa Barb. Rodr.

Pendare .... Couma macrocarpa Barb. Rodr. and Couma utilis
(Mart.) Muell Arg.

Perillo... Couma macrocarpa Barb. Rodr. and Couma utilis
(Mart.) Muell Arg.

Moraceae:

Leche de vaca .... Brosimum utile (H.S.K.) Pittier and Poulsenia spp
Lacmellea standleyi (Woodson), Monachino (Apocynaceae).

Niger gutta .... Ficus platyphylla Del.

Tunu (tuno) .... Castilla fallax Cook.

Euphorbiaceae:

Chilte .... Cnidoscolus (also known as Jatropha) elasticus Lundell
and Cnidoscolus tepiquensis (cost. and Gall.) McVaugh.

SYNTHETIC

SPECIFICATIONS

Butadiene-styrene rubber .... Basic polymer.

Isobutylene-isoprene copolymer
(butyl rubber). .... Do.

Paraffin .... Synthesized by Fischer-Tropsch process from carbon
monoxide and hydrogen, which are catalytically converted
to a mixture of paraffin hydrocarbons. Lower molecular weight fractions
are removed by distillation. The resudue is hydrogenated and further
treated by percolation through activated charcoal. The product has a
congealing point of 200°F-210°F as determined by A.S.T.M. D-938-49 method;
a maximum oil content of by A.S.T.M. D-721-56t method; and an
absorptivity of less than 0.01 at 290 millimicrons in decahene at
190°F as determined by A.S.T.M. D-2008 method.

Petroleum wax ....Complying with § 172,886.

Petroleum wax synthetic ....Complying with §172,888.

Polyeethylene .... Molecular weight 2,000-21,000

Polyisobutylene ....Minimum molecular weight 37,000 (Flory).

Polyvinyl acetate .... Molecular weight, minimum 2,000.

PLASTICIZING MATERIALS (SOFTENERS)

Glycerol ester of partially dimerized rosin..Having an acid number of 3-8, a drop-softening
point of 109° C-119°C. and a color of M or paler.

MASTICATORY SUBSTANCES (Continued)
NATURAL (COAGULATED OR CONCENTRATED LATICES) OF VEGETABLE ORIGIN

Glycerol ester of partially hydrogenated
gum or wood rosin .... Having an acid number of 3-10, a drop-softening
point of 79° C-88°C. and a color of N or paler.

Glycerol ester of polymerized rosin .... Having an acid number of 3-12, a melting point
range of 80° C-126°C. and a color of M or paler.

Glycerol ester of gum rosin .... Having an acid number of 5-9, a drop-softening
point of 88° C-96°C. and a color of N or paler.
The ester is purified by steam stripping.

Glycerol ester of tall oil rosin .... Having an acid number of 2-12, a drop-softening
point (ring and ball) of 80° C-88°C. and a color of N or paler.
The ester is purified by steam stripping.

Glycerol ester of wood rosin .... Having an acid number of 3-9, a drop-softening
point of 88° C-96°C. and a color of N or paler.
The ester is purified by steam stripping.

Lanolin ....
Methyl ester of rosin, partially hydrogenated...Having an acid number of 4-8, a refractive index
of 1.5170-1.5205 at 20°C, and a viscosity of 23-66 poises at 25°.
The ester is purified by steam stripping.

Pentaerythritol ester of partially
hydrogenated gum or wood resin .... Having an acid number of 7-18, a drop-softening
point of 102° C-110°C. and a color of K or paler.

Pentaerythritol ester of gum
or wood rosin .... Having an acid number of 6-16, a drop-softening
point of 109° C-116°C. and a color of M or paler.

Rice bran wax .... Complying with §172,890.
Stearic acid .... Complying with §172,860.
Sodium and potassium stearates .... Complying with §172,863.

TERPENE RESINS

Synthetic resin .... Consisting of polymers of a-pinene, b-pinene, and/or
dipentene; acid value less than 5, saponification number less than 5,
and a color less than 4 on the gardner s 50 percent mineral spirit solution.

Natural resin .... Consisting of polymers of a-pinene; softening point
minimum 155°c, determined by U.S.P. closed-capillary method,
United States Pharmacopeia XX (1980) (page 961)

ANTIOXIDANTS

Butylated hydroxyanisole .... Not to exceed antioxidant content of 0.1% when used
alone or in any combination.

Butylated hydroxytoluene .... Do.
Propyl gallate .... Do.

MISCELLANEOUS

Sodium sulfate ....
Sodium sulfide .... Reaction-control agent in synthetic polymer production.

DAIRY PRODUCTS

T he standard for the designation "dairy" for kashrus purposes is different from the government standard. Many products approved by the government as "non-dairy" are actually dairy according to Jewish law. (See also "Non-dairy products," page 134). A common example of this is "non-dairy creamer." Even when this product is certified kosher, we often will find an O/U$_D$ or O/K$_D$, as these products often contains casein, a milk derivative.

Three classes of dairy ingredients exist:

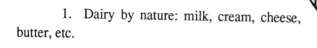

1. Dairy by nature: milk, cream, cheese, butter, etc.

2. Milk derivatives: casein, lactalbumin (see albumin), lactose, potassium caseinate, sodium caseinate, whey. (Lactic acid is pareve unless it is used in a dairy product.)

3. Dairy by contamination from equipment and utensils: many baked goods, chocolates, margarine.

Products that need to be checked carefully because they regularly contain the above ingredients are: margarine, "non-dairy" products, baked goods (cookies, pretzels, cake mixes, etc.), and breakfast cereals.

Dairy foods such as yogurt, sour cream, and whipping cream require supervision. Common problems: gelatin, emulsifiers, stabilizers, flavors, colors.

Products such as sour cream, buttermilk, cottage cheese, and others require supervision. Common problem: rennet and gelatin.

FISH

ish which have fins and scales are kosher. Fish which only have fins are not kosher. Of the four types of scales, clenoid, cycloid, ganoid and placoid, only clenoid and cycloid scales are valid according to the Torah. Gandoid is the type found on sturgeon and placoid is found on shark. There is no prohibition against eating fish blood, other than the fact that people may think that a person is eating prohibited blood, and ritual slaughter is not required.

The scales must be true scales that can be removed without damaging the skin of the fish. As it says in the Torah – "These you may eat of the fishes, all that have fins and scales..." (Vayikrah XI:9-12) Bony tubercles and plate or thorn-like scales that can be removed only by removing part of the skin are not considered scales in this context. Some fish that have such scales, such as eels, lumpfish, shark, sturgeon, and swordfish, are not kosher. All shellfish and mammals (such as whales, and dolphins) are not kosher. Only the eggs of kosher fish, such as fish roe or caviar, are allowed, therefore supervision is necessary. Care must be taken when buying fresh, whole fish, filleted, or frozen, because of the possibility of substitution by non-kosher fish or of contamination by remnants of non-kosher fish from knives and cutting boards. Fish sticks have three problems: the fish, the oil, and the frying utensils and equipment (which is usually used for non-kosher fish as well as kosher fish).

Smoked fish is frequently soaked in brine and then smoked along with non-kosher fish. According to Jewish law, this soaking and smoking is tantamount to cooking over a flame and therefore the product is not kosher. Smoked fish is also often packed in oil, which may not be kosher.

Although herring is famous as a Jewish food, it is not always kosher. The preparation of herring can pose a myriad of problems among which are mono- and di-glycerides, non-kosher wine vinegar or wine, sour cream, bread crumbs, spices, and equipment contamination.

These lists of kosher and non-kosher fish were prepared by James W. Atz, Ph.D., Curator and Dean Bibliographer in the Department of

Ichthyology of the American Museum of Natural History, New York, New York 10024.

I would like to thank Rabbi Genack and the Union of Orthodox Jewish Congregations of America for allowing us to reprint this list.

KOSHER FISH

Albacore See: Mackerels
Alewife See: Herrings
Amberjack See: Jacks
Anchovies (Family Engraulidae). Including: European anchovy (Engraulis encrasciolus), North of California anchovy (Engraulis mordax).
Angelfishes and butterfly fishes (Family Chaetodontidae). Including: Angelfishes (Holacanthus species, Pomacanthus species).
Atlantic Pomfret or Ray's Bream (Brama brama)
Ballyhoo See: Flyingfishes
Barracudas (Family Sphyraenidae) Including: Barracudas and kakus (Sphyraena species).
Bass See: Sea Basses. Temperate basses, Sunfishes, Drums
Bigeyes (Family Priacanthidae). Including: Bigeyes or aweoweos (Priacanthus species).
Blackfish See: Carps, Wrasses
Blacksmith See: Damselfishes
Blueback See: Flounders, Herrings, Trouts
Bluefish or snapper blue (Pomatomus saltarix)
Bluegill See: Sunfishes
Bocaccio See: Scorpionfishes
Bombay duck (Harpadeon nehereus)
Bonefish (Albula vulpes)
Bonito See: Cobia, Mackerels
Bowfin Freshwater dogfish, or grindle (Amia calva)
Bream See: Carps, Atlantic pomfret, Porgies
Brill See: Flounder

Buffalo fishes See: Suckers

Burbot See: Codfishes

Butterfishes (Family Stromateidae), Including: Butterfish (Peprilus tracanthus); Pacific pompano (Peprilus similimus); harvestfishes (Peprilus species)

Butterfly fish See: Angelfish

Cabrilla See: Sea Basses

Calico bass See: Sunfishes

Capelin See: Smelts

Carps and minnows (Family Cyprinidae), Including: the carp, leather carp, mirror carp (Cyprinus carpio); Crucian carp (Carassius carassius); Goldfish (Carassius auratus); tench (Tinca tinca); Splittail (Pogonichthys macrolepidotus); Squawfishes (Ptychocheilus species); Scramento backfish or hardhead (Orthodon microlepidotus); Freshwater breams (Abramis species, Blicca species); Roach (Rutilus rutilus).

Carosucker See: Suckers

Caviar (Must be from a kosher fish) See: Trouts and whitefishes (salmon), Lumpsuckers (non-kosher), Sturgeons (non-kosher).

Cero See: Mackerels

Channel bass See: Drums

Char See: Trouts

Chilipepper See: Scorpionfishes

Chinook salmon See: Trouts

Chup See: Trouts, Sea chubs

Cichlids (Family Chichilidae), Including: Tilapias (Tilapia species); Mozambique mouthbrooder (Tilapia mossambica); Cichlios (Cichlasoma species); Rio Grande perch (Cichlasoma cyanoguttatum)

Cigarfish See: Jacks

Cisco See: Trouts

Coalfish See: Codfishes

Cobia, cabio, or black bonito (Rachycentron canadum)

Cod, cultus, black, blue, or ling. See: Greenlings, Sablefish

Codfishes (Family Gadidae), Including: Cod (Gadus morhua), Haddock (Melanogrammus aegiefinus); Pacific cod (Gadus macrocephalus); Pollock, saithe, or coalfish (Pollachius virens); Walleye pollock (Theragra chalcogramma); Hakes (Urophycis species); Whiting (Meriangius meriangus); Blue whiting or poutassou (Micromesistius poutassou); Burbot, lawyer, or freshwater ling (Iota Iota); Tomcods or frostfishes (Microgradus species).

Coho salmon See: Trouts

Corbina or Corvina, See: Drums

Cottonwick See: Grunts

Crapplie See: Sunfishes

Creville See: Jacks

Croacker See: Drums

Crucian carp See: Carps

Cubbyu See: Drums

Cunner See: Wrasses

Dab See: Flounders

Damselfishes (Family Pomacentridae). Including: Blacksmith (Chromis punctipinnis); Garibaldi (Hypsypops rubicunda).

Doctorfish See: Surgeonfishes

Dolly Varden See: Trouts

Dolphin fishes or mahimahis (Coryphaena species) Not to be confused with the Mammal called Dolphin or Porpoise, which is non-kosher.

Drums and croakers (Family Sciaenidae), Including: Seatrouts and carvinas (Cynoscion species); Weakfish (Cynoscion nebulosus); White seabass (Cynoscion nobillis); Croakers (micropogon species, Bairdiella species, Odontoscion species); Silver perch (Bairdiella chyrsura); White or King croaker (Genyonemus lineatus); Black croaker (cheilottena saturnum); Spotfin croaker (Roncador stearnsi); Yellowfin croaker (Umbrina roncador); Drums (Pogonias species, Stellifer species, Umbrina species); Red drum or channel bass (Sciaenops ocallata); Freshwater drum (Aplodinotus grunniens); Kingfishes or king whitings (Menticirrhus species); California corbina (Menticirrhus undulatus); spot or lafayette (Leiostomus xanthurus); Queenfish (Seriphus politus); Cubbyu or ribbon fish (Equetus umbrosus).

Eulachon See: Smelts

Flounders (Families Bothidae and Pleuronectidae). Including: Flounders (Paralichthys species, Liopsetta species, Platichthys species,etc.); Starry flounder (Platichthys stellatus); Summer flounder or fluke (Paralichthys denatus); Yellowtail flounder (limanda ferrugina); Winter flounder, lemon sole or blackback (Pseudopleuronectes americanus); Halibuts (Hippoglossus species); California halibut (Paralichthys Californicus); Bigmouth sole (Hippoglossina stomata); Butter of scalyfin sole (Isopsetta isolepis); "Dover" sole (Microstomus pacificus); "English" sole (Parophrys vetulus); Fantail sole (Xystreurys liolepis); Petrale sole (Eopsetta jordan); Rex sole (Glyptocephalus zichirus); Rock sole (Lepidopsetta bilineata); Sand Sole (Psettichthys melanostictus); Slender sole (Lyopsetta exillis); Yellowfin sole (Limanda aspera); Pacific turbots (Pleuronichthys species); Curlfin turbot or sole (Pleuronichthys decurrens); Diamond turbot (Hypsopsetta guttulata); Greenland turbot or halibut (Reinhardtius hippoglossoides); Sanddabs (Citharichthys species); Dabs (Limanda species); American plaice (Hippoglossoides platessoides); European plaice (Pleuronectes platessa); Brill (scophthalmus rhomus). But not including: European turbot (Scophthalmus maximus or Psetta maximus).

Fluke See: Flounders

Flyingfishes and halfbeaks (Family Exocoetidae); Flyingfishes (Cypselurus species, and others); Ballyhoo or balao (Hemiramphus species).

Frostfish See: Codfishes

Gag See: Sea basses

Garibaldi See: Damselfishes

Giant kelpfish (Heterostichus rostratus)

Gizzard shad See: Herrings

Goatfishes or surmullets (Family Mullidae). Including: Goatfishes (Mullus species, Pseudupeneus species); Wekes or goatfishes (Mulloidichthys species, Upeneus species); Kumu (Parupeneus species); Red mullet (Mullus surmuletus).

Gobies (Family Gobidae), Including: Bigmouth sleeper or guavina (Gobiomorus dormitor); Sirajo goby (sicydium plumieri)

Goldeye and mooneye (Hiodon alosoides and Hiodon tergisus).

Goldfish See: Carps

Grayling See: Trouts

Graysby: See: Sea basses

Greenlings (Family Hexagrammidae), Including: Greenlings (Hexagrammos species); Kelp greenling or seatrout (Hexagrammos decagrammus); Lingcod, cultus or blue cod (Ophiodon elongatus); Atka mackerel (Pleurogrammus monopterygius).

Grindle See: Bowfin

Grouper See: Sea basses

Grunion See: Silversides

Grunts (Family Pomadasyldae), Including; Grunts (Haemulon species, Pomadasys species); Margate (Haemulon album); Tomtate (Haemulon aurolineattum); Cottonwick (Haemulon melanurum); Sailors choice (Haemulon parral); Porkfish (Anisotremus virginicus); Black margate (Anisotremus surinamensis); Sargo (Anisotremus davidsoni); Pigfish (Orthopristis chrysoptera).

Guavina See: Gobies

Haddock See: Codfishes

Hake See also Codfishes

Hakes (Family Meriucciidae), Including: Hakes (Merluccius species); Silver hake or whiting (Meriuccius bilinearis); Pacific hake or meriuccio (Meriuccius productus)

Halfbeak See: Flying fish

Halfmoon See: Sea chubs

Halibut See: Flounders

Hamlet See: Sea basses

Hardhead See: Carps

Harvestfish See: Butterfishes

Hawkfishes (Family Cirrhitidae). Including: Hawkfishes (Cirrhitus species).

Herrings (Family Clupeidae), Including: Atlantic and Pacific herring (Clupae harengus subspecies); thread herrings (Opisthonema species); Shads (Alosa species); Shad or glut herring, or blueback (Alosa aestivalis); Hickory shad (Alosa mediocris); Alewife or river herring (Alosa pseudoharengus); Gizzard shads (Dorosoma species); Menhadens or mossbunkers (Brevoortia species); Spanish sardines (Sardineila anchovia); European sardine or pilchard (Sardina pilchardus); Pacific sardine or pilchard (Sardinops sagax); Spart (Sprattus sprattus)

Hind See: Sea bass

Hogchocker See: Soles

Hogfish See: Wrasses

Horse mackerel See: Jacks

Jack Mankerel See: Jacks

Jacks and Pompanos (Family Charangidae) Including: Pompanos, palometas, and permits (Trachionotus species); Amberjacks and yellowtails (Seriola species); California yellowtail (Seriola dorsalls); Scads and cigarfish (Decapterus species, Selar species, Trachurus species); Jack mackerel or horse mackerel (Trachurus symmetricus); Jacks and uluas (Caranx species, Carangoides species); Crevalles (Caranx species); Blue runner (Caranx crysos); Rainbow runner (Elagatis bipinnulata); Moonfishes (Vomer species); Lookdown (Selene vomer); Leatherback or lae (Scomberoides sanctipetri); BUT NOT INCLUDING: Leatherjacket (Oligoplites saurus).

Jacksmelt See: Silversides

Jewfish See: Sea basses.

John Dory (Zeus faber)

Kelpfish See: Giant Kelpfish

Kingfish See: Drums, mackerels

Ladyfish, or tenpounder (Elops saurus)

Lafayette See: Drums

Lake Herring See: Trouts

Lance or Launce See: Sand lances

Largemouth bass See: Sunfishes

Lawyer See: Codfishes

Leatherback See: Jacks

Lingcod See: Greenlings

Lizardfishes (Family Synodontidae)

Lookdown See: Jacks

Mackerel See also: Jacks

Mackerels, Atka See: Greenlings

Mackerels and tunas (Family Scombridae), Including: Mackerels (Scomber species, Scomberomorus species, Auxis species); Spanish mackerels, cero, and sierra (Scomberomorus species); King mackerel or kingfish (Scomberomorus cavalla); Bonitos (Sarda species); Wahoo (Acanthocybius solanderi); tunas (Thunnus species, Euthynnus species); Skipjack tunas (Euthynnus or Katsuwonus species); Albacore (thunnus alalunga) But not including: Snake mackerels

Mahimahi See: Dolphin fishes

Margate See: Grunts

Menhaden See: Herrings

Menpachii See: Squirrelfishes

Merluccio See: Hakes

Milkfish or awa (Chanos chanos)

Mojarras (Family Gerreidae) including: Mojarras (Eucinostomus species, Gerres species, Diapterus species)

Monkeyface prickleback or eel (Cebidichthys violaceus)

Mooneye See: Goldeye

Moonfish See: Jacks

Mossbunker See: Herrings

Mouthbrooder See: Cichlids

Mullet See: Goatfishes

Mullets (Family Mugilidae) including: Mullets and amaamas (Mugil species); Uouoa (Neomyxus chaptallii); Mountain mullets or dajaos (agonostomus species)

Muskellunge See: Pikes

Mutton hamlet See: Sea basses

Muttonfish See: Snappers

Needlefishes (Family Beslonidae) Needlefishes or marine gars (strongylura species, Tylosuru species)

Opaleye See: Sea clubs

Palometa See: Jacks

Parrotfishs (Family Scaridae) including: Parrotfishes and uhus (Scarus species, Slparisoma species)

Perch See also: Temperate basses, Drums, Cichlids, Surfperches, Scorpionfishes

Perches (Family Percidae) including: Yellow perch (Perca flavescens); Walleye, pike-perch, or yellow or blue pike (Stizostedion vitreum); Sauger (Stizostedion canadense)

Permit See: Jacks

Pickerel See: Pike

Pigfish See: Grunts

Pike See also: Perches

Pikes (Family Esocidae) including; Pike (esox lucius); Pickerels (Esox species); Muskellunge (esox masquinongy)

Pike-perch See: Perches

Pilchard See Herrings

Pinfish See: Porgies

Plaice See: Flounders

Pollock. See: Codfishes

Pomfret. See: Atlantic pomfret

Pompano See: Jack, Butterfishes

Porgies and sea breams (Family Sparidae). Including: Porgies (Calamus species, Diplodus species, Pagrus species); Scup (Stenotomus chrysops); Pinfish (Lagodon rhomboides); Sheepshead (Archosargus probatocephalus)

Porkfish See: Gruntts

Poutassou See: Codfishes

Prickleback See: Monkeyface prickleback, Rockprickleback (non-kosher).

Queenfish See: Drums

Quillback See: Suckers

Rabalo See: Snooks

Ray's bream See: Atlantic pomfret

Red snapper See: Snappers

Redfish See: Scorpionfishes, Wrasses

Roach See: Carps

Rock bass See: Sunfishes

Rockhind See: Sea basses

Rockfish See: Scorpionfishes. Temperate basses

Rosefish See: Scorpionfishes

Rudderfish See: Sea chubs

Runner See: Jack

Sablefish or black cod (Anoplopoma fimbria)

Sailors choice See: Grunts

Saithe See: Codfishes

Salmon See: Trouts

Sand lances, launces, or eels (Ammodytes species)

Sardine See: Herrings

Sargo See: Grunts

Sauger See: Perches

Scad See: Jacks

Scamp See: Sea basses

Schoolmaster See: Snappers

Scorpionfishes (family Scorpaenidae), Including: Scorpionfishes (Scorpaena species); California scorpionfish or sculpin (Scorpaena guttata); Nohus (Scorpaenopsis species); Redfish, rosefish, or ocean perch (Sebasters marinus); rockfishes (Sebasters species, Sebastodes species); Pacific ocean perch (Sebastes alutus); Chilipepper (Sebastes goodel); Bocaccio (Sebastes paucipinus); Shortspine thornyhead or channel rockfish (Sebastolobus alascanus)

Scup See: Porgies

Sea bass See also: Temperate basses, drums

Sea basses (Family Serranidae) including: Black sea basses (Centropristis species); Groupers (Epinephelus species, and Mycteroperca species); Rockhind (Epinephelus adscensionis); Speckled hind (Epinephelus drummondhayi); Red hind (Epinephelus guttatus); Jewfish (Epinephelus itajara); Spotted cabrilla (Epinephelus analogus); Gag (Mycteroperca microlepis); Scamp (Mycteroperca phenax); Graysby (petrometopon cruentatum); Mutton hamlet (Alphestes afer) Sand bass, kelp bass, and spotted bass (Paralabrax species)

Sea bream See: Porgies

Sea chubs (Family Kyphosidae) including: Bermuda chug or rudderfish (Kyphosus sectatrix); Opaleye (Girella nigrican); Halfmoon (Medialuna californiensis)

Seaperch See: Surfperches

Searobins (Family Triglidae); Searobins (Prionotus species)

Seatrout See: Drums, Greenlings, Steelhead

Shad See: Herrings

Sheepshead See: Porgies, Wrasses

Sierra See: Mackerels

Silversides (Family Athernidae) including: Whitebait, spearing, or silversides (Menidia species); California grunion (Leurusthes tenuis); Jacksmelt (Atherinopsis californiensis); Topsmelt (Atherinops affinis)

Sirajo goby See: Gobies

Skipjack See Mackerels

Sleeper See Gobies

Smallmouth bass See Sunfishes

Smelts (Family Osmeridae) including: Smelts (Osmerus species); Capelin (Malotus villosus); Eullachon (Thaleichthys pacificus)

Snapper blue See: Bluefish

Snappers (Family Lutjanidae) including: Snappers (Lutjanus species); Schoolmaster (Lutjanus apodus); Muttonfish or mutton snapper (Lutjanus analis); Red snapper (Lutjanus campechanus); Yellowtail snapper (Ocyurus chrysurus); Kalikali (Pristipomoides sieboldi); Opakapaka (Pristipomoides microlepis); Onaga (Etelis carbunculus)

Snooks (Family Centropomidae) including: Snooks or rabalos (Centropomus species)

Sockeye salmon See: Trouts

Sole See also: Flounders

Soles (Family Soleidae), Including: Sole or true sole (solea solea); Lined sole (Achirus lineatus); Hogchoker (Trinectes maculatus).

Spadefishes (Family Ephippidae). Including: Spadefishes (Chaetodipterus species)

Spanish mackerel See: Mackerels

Spearing See: Silversides

Splitttail See: Carps

Spot See: Drums

Sprat See: Herrings

Squawfish See: Carp

Squirrelfishes (Family Holocentridae), Including: Squirrelfishes (Holocentrus species); Menpachii (Myripristis species).

Steelhead See: Trouts

Striped bass See: Temperate basses

Suckers (Family Catostomidae). Including: Buffalo fishes (Ictiobus species); Suckers (Catostomus species, Moxostoma species); Quillbacks or carpsuckers (Carpiodes species)

Sunfishes (Family Centrarchidae). Including: Freshwater basses (Micropterus species); Largemouth bass (Microterus salmoides); Smallmouth bass (Micropterus dolomieui); Sunfishes (Lepomis species); Bluegill (Lepomis macrochirus); Warmouth (Lepomis macrochirus); Rock bass or red eye (Ambloplites rupestris); Crappies or calico basses (Pomoxis species)

Surfperches (Famly Embiotocidae). Including: Surfperches (Amphistichus species, Hyperprosopon species); Seaperches (Embiotoca species, Hypsurus species, Phanerodon species, Rhacochilus species); Black perth (Embiotoca jacksoni); Pile perch (Rhacochilus vacca); Shiner perch (Cymatogaster aggregata). **Surgeonfishes** (Family Acanthuridae). Including: Surgeonfishes and tangs (Acanthurus species, Zebrasoma species); Doctorfish (Acanthurus chirugus); Unicornfishes or kalas (Naso species).

Tang See: Surgeonfishes

Tarpon (Megalops atlantica)

Tautog See: Wrasses

Temperate basses (Family Percichthyidae). Including: Striped bass or rockfish (morone saxatillis); Yellow bass (Morone mississippiensis); White bass (Morojne chrysops); White perch (Morone americana); Giant California sea bass (Stereolepis gigas)

Tench See: Carps

Tenpounder See Ladyfish

Threadfins (Family polynemidae) including: Blue bobo (Polydactylus approximans); Barbu (Polydactylus virginicus); Moi (Polydactylus sexfilis)

Tilapia See: Cichlids

Tilefishes (Family Branchiostegidae) including: tilefish (Logholatilus chamaeleonticeps) Ocean whitefish (Caulolatilus princeps)

Tomcod See: Codfishes

Tomtate See: Grunts

Tomsmelt See: Silversides

Tripletail (Lobotes surinamensis)

Trouts and whitefishes (Family Salmonidae) including: Atlantic salmon (Salmo salar); Pacific salmons (Oncorhtnchus species); Coho or silver salmon; sockeye, blueback or red salmon; chinook, king or spring salmon; pink or humpback salmon; chum, dog or fall salmon, Trouts (Salmo species) Brown trout, rainbow trout or steelhead, cutthroat trout, golden trout, Chars (Salvelinus species); Lake trout, brook rout, Arctic char, Dolly Varden, Whitefishes and ciscos (coregonus species and Prosopium species); Cisco or lake herring (Corengonus artedii); chubs (coregonus species); graylings (thymallus Species)

Tuna See: Mackerels

Turbot See Flounder (some non-kosher)

Unicornfish See: Surgeonfishes

Wahoo See: Mackerels

Walleye See: Perches

Walleye pollock See: Codfishes

Warmouth See: Sunfishes

Weakfishes See: Drums

Whitefish See: Trouts, Tilefishes

Whiting See: Codfishes, Hakes, Drums

Wrasses (Family Labridae) including: Hogfishes and aawas (Bodianus species); Hogfish or capitaine (Lachnolaimus maximus); Tautog or blackfish (Tautoga onitis); California sheephead or redfish (Pimelometopon pulchrum); Cunner, chogset, or bergall (Tautogolabrus adspersus)

Yellowtail See: Jacks

Yellowtail snapper See Snappers

NON-KOSHER FISH

Angler See: Goosefishes

Beluga See: Sturgeons

Billfishes (Family Istiophoridae). Including fishes (Istiophorus species); Marlins and spea ishes (Tetrapterus species, Makaira species).

Blowfish See: Puffers

Bullhead See: Catfishes

Cabezon See: Sculpins

Catfishes (Order Siluriformes). Including: Channel catfish (Ictalurus punctatus); Bullheads (Ictalurus species); Sea catfish (Arius felis)

Cutlassfishes (Family Trichiuridae) including: Cutlassfishes (Trichiurus species) Scabbardfishes (Lepidopus species)

Dogfish See: Bowfin, Sharks

Eels (Order Anguilliforms). Including American and European eel (Anguilia rostrata and Anguila anguila); Conger eel (Conger oceanicus).

Gars (Order Semionotiformes). Freshwater gars (Lepisosteus species).

Goosefishes or anglers (Lophius species)

Grayfish See: Sharks

Lampreys (Family Petromyzontidae)

Leatherjacket See: Jacks (Oligoplites saurus)

Lomosuckers (Family Cyclopteridae). Including: Lumpfish (Cyclopterus lumpus); Snailfishes (Liparis species).

Marlin See: Billfishes

Midshipman See: Toadfishes

Ocean pout or eelpout (Macrozoarces americanus)

Oilfish (Ruvettus pretiosus) Puffers (Family Tetraodontidae).

Paddlefish See: Sturgeons

Pout See: Ocean pout

Puffers, blowfishes, swellfishes, sea squab (Sphoeroides species)

Ratfish See: Sharks

Ray See: Sharks

Rock prickleback or rockeel (Xiphister mucosus)

Sailfish See: Billfishes

Sculpins (Family Cottidae). Including: Sculpins (Myoxocephalus species, Cottus species, Leptocottus species, etc.). Cabezon (Scorpaenichthys marmoratus); Searaven (Hemitripterus americanus)

Searaven See: Sculpins

Sea-squab See: Puffers

Sharks, rays and their relatives (Class Chondrichthyes). Including Grayfishes or dogfishes (Mustelus species, Squalus species); Soupfin shark (Galeorhinus zyopterus); Sawfishes (Pristis species); Skates (Raja species); Chimaeras or ratfishes (Order Chimaeriformes).

Skates See: Sharks

Snake mackerels (Gempylus species)

Spoonbill cat See: Sturgeons

Sturgeons (Order Acipenseriformes). Including: Sturgeons (Acipensen species, Scaphirhynchus species); Beluga (huso uso); Paddrefish or spoonbill cat (Polyodon spathula)

Swordfish (Xiphias gladies)

Toadfishes (Family Batrachoididae). Including: Toadfishes (Opsanus species); Midshipment (Porichthys species).

Tiggerfishes and firefishes (Family Balistidae). Triggerfishes (Balistes species, Canthidermis species)

Trunkfishes (Family Ostraciidad). Trunkfishes and cowfishes (Lactophrys species).

Wolffishes (Family Anarhichadidae). Including: Wolffishes or ocean. catfishes (Anarhichas species)

Multilingual Guide to Common Names of Some Kosher Saltwater Fishes

Following are the common names, in several different languagesof some Kosher fish. The names are those applied in the areas where the species occur or are commonly known. The species are listed alphabetically according to the English standard common name.

ALBACORE
French: germon
German: Weisser Thun
Hawaiian: àhipalaha
Italian: alalonga
Japanese: bin'naga, binnagamaguro, binchô, tombo
Portuguese: voador, albacora, albacora branca
Spanish: albacora, atún blanco, bonito del norte

BARRACUDA, great
French: barracuda, bécune, brochet de mer
German: Grosser Barrakuda
Hawaiian: kaku
Italian: barracuda, sfirena
Japanese: onikamasu
Portuguese: barracuda, bicuda americana
Spanish: barracuda, picua, picúda, bicuda, espetón, picúa brava, picúa corsaria, picúa zorra

BASS, European
French: bar
German: Seebarsch, Wolfsbarsch
Italian: spigola
Spanish: lubina

BASS, giant sea
French: merou géant du Pacifique
Japanese: ishinagi-zoku
Spanish: mero gigante del Pacifico, cherna, lubina marina gigante

BASS, striped
Spanish: lobina rayada, lobina barrada, lubina listada

BLUEFISH
French: tassergal, balarin
German: Blaufisch, Wolfsbarsch
Italian: pesce serra, ballerino
Japanese: amikiri, okisuzuki, okisade
Portuguese: anchova, enchova
Spanish: anchoa, anjova

BONITO, Atlantic
French: bonite à dos rayé
German: Bonito, Pelamide
Italian: palamita
Japanese: hagatsuo-rui
Portuguese: serrajao
Spanish: bonito (del Atlántico), carachana

BONITO, Pacific
Japanese: hagatsuo, kitsunegatsuo
Spanish: bonito (del Pacifico)

COD, Atlantic & Pacific
French: morue, cabillaud, fraiche, morue franche
German: Kabeljau, Dorsch
Italian: merluzzo bianco
Japanese: madara, tara-ka
Portuguese: bacalhau
Spanish: bacalao, bacallao

DOLLY VARDEN
Russian: malma

DOLPHIN
French: coryphene, dauphin
Hawaiian: mahi mahi
Italian: corifena, lampuga, pappagallo
Japanese: shiira
Portuguese: dourado
Spanish: dorado, lampugus, llampugas, peje vapor

HALIBUT, Atlantic
French: flétan de l'Atlantique
German: Heilbutt

HALBUT, Pacific
Japanese: ohyo-rui

JEWFISH
Portuguese: mero, garoupa
Spanish: mero, cherna, guasa, mero sapo, mero-cherna, mero brasil, pez judío

MACKEREL, king
Portuguese: cavala real, serra
Spanish: carite rey, caballa real, sierra, carita, sierra grande, sierra de altura, sierra canalera, carite lucio

MACKEREL, Spanish
Spanish: sierra, carite pintado

PERCH, white
French: bar-perche

POLLACK
French: lieu jaune, colin jaune
German: Pollack
Italian: merluzzo giallo
Portuguese: badejo, juliana
Spanish: abadejo

POLLOCK
French: lieu noir, colin, merlan noire, goberge
German: Kohler, Seelachs
Portuguese: escamudo
Spanish: abadejo, abadejo negro, badejo

SALMON, chinook
Russian: Tshawytscha

SALMON, chum
Russian: keta

SALMON, coho
Russian: kisutch

SALMON, pink
Fiussian: gorbuscha

SALMON, sockeye
Russian: nerka

SEABASS, Japanese
Japanese: suzuki

SEABASS, blackfin
Japanese: hira-suzuki

SEABASS, white
Spanish: cabaicucho, corvina blanca, pescadilla

TROUT, brook
French: truite

TROUT, lake
French: touladi

TUNA, bigeye
French: thon obese, patudo, thon ventru
Hawaiian: po'o-nui, ahipo'o-nui
Japanese: mebachi, shibi
Portuguese: patudo
Spanish: atun ojo grande, patudo

TUNA, blackfin
Japanese: taiseiyômaguro
Portuguese: albacorinha, atum-preto
Spanish: atún aleta negra, atún aletinegro, albacora

TUNA, bluefin
French: thon touge
German: Blauflossenthun, Roter Thun
Italian: tonno
Japanese: kuromaguro, hon-maguro, maguro
Portuguese: atum, atum-azul
Spanish: atún aleta azul, atun gigante, atún rojo

TUNA, dogtooth
French: thon blanc
Japanese: isomaguro

TUNA, longtail
Japanese: koshinaga

TUNA, skipjack
French: bonite à ventre rayé
Hawaiian: aku
Italian: tonnetto striato
Japanese: katsuo

Portuguese: gaiado, listao, listado
Spanish: listado, bonito artico, barrilete

TUNA, southern bluefin
French: thon (rouge) du sud, thon rouge austral
Japanese: minamimaguro

TUNA, yellowfin
French: albacore, thon à nageoires jaunes
German: Gelbflossenthun
Hawaiian: ahi, ahimalailena malailena
Italian: albacore, tonno albacora
Japanese: kihada, kiwade, kiwada maguro
Portuguese: albacora, atum amarello
Spanish: atun de aleta amarilla, atún de Allison, rabil

WHITEFISH, lake
French: grand coregone

YELLOWTAIL, California
Spanish: jurel de Castilla, colarubia, colirubia, pez limon, seriola de California

YELLOWTAIL, southern
French: sériole australe, liche
Portuguese: seriola do sul, olhete, charuteiro
Spanish: jurel de Castilla, colarubia, colirubia, pez limón, seriola austral

ILLUSTRATIONS OF SOME POPULAR KOSHER FISH

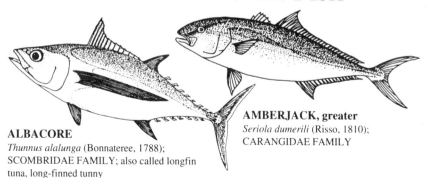

AMBERJACK, greater
Seriola dumerili (Risso, 1810);
CARANGIDAE FAMILY

ALBACORE
Thunnus alalunga (Bonnateree, 1788);
SCOMBRIDAE FAMILY; also called longfin
tuna, long-finned tunny

BASS, giant sea
Stereolepis gigas (Ayres, 1859);
THYIDAE FAMILY; also
called California black sea bass,
California jewfish

BASS, black sea
Centropristis striata (Linnaeus, 1758);
RANIDAE FAMILY; also called sea bass,
black bass, rockbass, common sea bass,
humpback (large males)

BASS, largemouth
Micropterus salmoides (Lacepede, 1802);
CENTRARCHIDAE FAMILY; also called
black bass, Oswego bass, green bass, green
trout, Florida bass, florida (or southern)
largemouth, northern largemouth

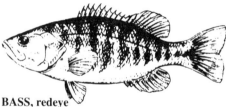

BASS, kelp (calico)
Paralabrax clathratus (Girard, 1854);
SERRANIDAE FAMILY; also called calico
bass, California kelp bass, rock bass, sand
bass, bull bass, kelp salmon, cabrilla

BASS, redeye
Micropterus coosae (Hubbs & Bailey, 1940);
CENTRARCHIDAE FAMILY; also called black
bass, shoal bass

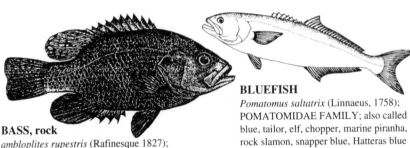

BASS, rock
ambloplites rupestris (Rafinesque 1827);
CENTRARCHIDAE FAMILY; also called black
perch, goggle-eye, red-eye, rock sunfish

BLUEFISH
Pomatomus saltatrix (Linnaeus, 1758);
POMATOMIDAE FAMILY; also called
blue, tailor, elf, chopper, marine piranha,
rock slamon, snapper blue, Hatteras blue

Pacific Bonito *(Sarda chiliensis)*

BONITO, Atlantic
Sarda sarda (Bloch, 1793);
SCOMBRIDAE FAMILY; also called common
bonito, katonkel, belted bonito

Striped Bonito *(Sarda orientalis)*

Australian Bonito *(Sarda australis)*

BONITO, Pacific
Sarda orientalis (Temminch & Schlegel, 1844);
Sarda chiliensis (Cuvier, 1831) and;
Sarda australis (Macleay, 1880)
SCOMBRIDAE FAMILY; also called Califor-
nia bonito, striped bonito, Australian bonito

BOWFISH
Amia calva (Linnaeus 1766);
AMIIDAE FAMILY; also called mudfish, mud
pike, dogfish, griddle, grinnel, cypress trout

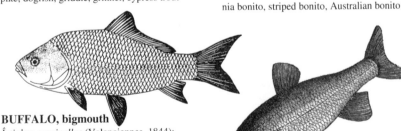

BUFFALO, bigmouth
Îctiobus cyprinellus (Valenciennes, 1844);
CATOSTOMIDAE FAMILY

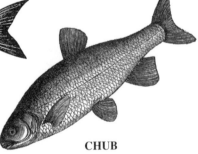

CHUB

CARP, common
Cyprinus carpio (Linnaeus 1758);
CYPRINIDAE FAMILY

186

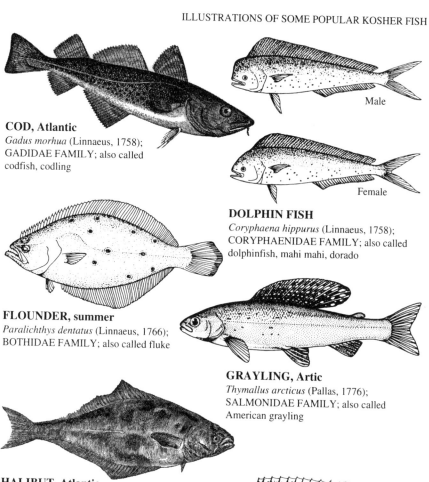

Male

Female

COD, Atlantic
Gadus morhua (Linnaeus, 1758);
GADIDAE FAMILY; also called
codfish, codling

DOLPHIN FISH
Coryphaena hippurus (Linnaeus, 1758);
CORYPHAENIDAE FAMILY; also called
dolphinfish, mahi mahi, dorado

FLOUNDER, summer
Paralichthys dentatus (Linnaeus, 1766);
BOTHIDAE FAMILY; also called fluke

GRAYLING, Artic
Thymallus arcticus (Pallas, 1776);
SALMONIDAE FAMILY; also called
American grayling

HALIBUT, Atlantic
Hippoglossus hippoglossus (Linnaeus 1758);
PLEURONECTIDAE FAMILY; also called
common halibut, giant halibut, righteye
flounder

JEWFISH
Epinephelus itajara (Lichtenstein, 1822);
SERRANIDAE FAMILY; also called
spotted jewfish, southern jewfish,
junefish, Florida jewfish

HERRING

LINGCOD
Ophiodon elongatus (Girard, 1854);
HEXAGRAMMIDAE FAMILY;
also called ling, cultus cod, green
cod, buffalo cod

PERCH, yellow
Perca flavescens (Mitchill, 1814);
PERCIDAE FAMILY; also called
lake perch, American perch, ringed perch,
striped perch, coon perch, jack perch

TROUT, lake
Salvelinus namaycush (Walbaum,
1792);
SALMONIDAE FAMILY; also
called
mackinaw, Great Lakes trout or
char, salmon trout, landlocked
salmon, gray trout, great gray
trout, mountain trout, laker,
tongue, taque, namaycush or
masamacush, siscowet, fat,
paperbelly, bank trout, humper

SALMON, coho
Oncorhynchus kisutch (Walbaum, 1792);
SALMONIDAE FAMILY; also called
silver salmon, silver sides, hooknose, sea
trout, blueback

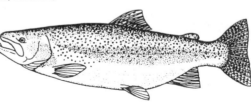

TROUT, rainbow
Oncorhynchus mykiss (Richardson, 1836);
SALMONIDAE FAMILY; also called
steelhead, Kamloops, redband trout, Eagle
Lake trout, Kern River trout, Shasta tro
Gorgonio trout, Nelson trout, Whitney
silver trout

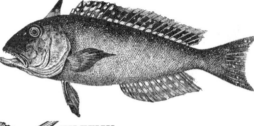

TILEFISH
Logholatilus chamaeleonticeps
BRANCHIOSTEGIDAE FAMILY; also
called ocean whitefish

TUNA, bluefin
Thunnus thynnus (Linnaeus 1758);
SCOMBRIDAE FAMILY; also called
Atlantic bluefin tuna, tunny fish, horse-
mackerel

ICE CREAM

S taying cool and kosher as the temperature rises requires an increased awareness and understanding of what may or may not be kashrus problems. Summertime products such as frozen desserts and yogurts, sodas, as well as other popular drinks and mixes usually contain ingredients that require supervision.

Ice creams, sherbets, frozen desserts, and ices contain a variety of emulsifiers, stabilizers, prepared mixes, and flavorings that require supervision. This is equally true of fruit ices and frozen ice pops which may contain a number of non-kosher stabilizers and flavorings. Sherbets and fruit sherbets contain milk by law and are **not** pareve. Ices also should not be considered as pareve unless endorsed as pareve on the product label.

Fortunately, throughout the United States, many companies have come to the economic realization that "Going Kosher" would increase their marketability. Today, many national brands of ices, ice creams and yogurts can be purchased with reliable certification at local supermarkets.

Each retail package of ice cream, ice milk, or sherbet has an ingredient listing of all ingredients on the label. This includes the ingredients in the flavors or other additives, which is parenthesized in the listing. Some of these labels become very complex due to these flavor ingredients.

Using flavored ice cream as an example, following is a breakdown of the ingredients and their sources:

Milkfat and Nonfat Milk: Includes the dairy ingredients such as milk, cream, and/or the condensed or dry equivalent.

Buttermilk: Is sweet cream buttermilk which is liquid remaining from the production of butter. It provides a high quality source of milk solids not fat.

Sugar: Is liquid or dry sugar and can be from a cane or beet source.

Corn Sweetener: Is liquid corn syrup which is a derivative of corn.

Guar Gum: Is a stabilizer which is from the guar seed, a legume grown in India.

Mono-diglycerides: Is an emulsifier which is derived from cotton-seed, palm, or coconut oils.

Polysorbate 80: Is also an emulsifier which is derived from cottonseed, palm or coconut oils.

Carob Bean Gum: Also known as Locust Bean Gum, is from the locust tree which is grown in the countries of Spain, Italy, and Greece.

Carrageenan: Also called Irish Moss is from seaweed, which is grown off the coasts of Massachusetts, Ireland, and France.

Natural and Artificial Flavors: In Vanilla flavored ice cream, this is the vanilla flavor which is a Category II flavoring made up of pure vanilla from the vanilla bean and an artificial vanilla flavor from vanillin.

Annatto Color: This is the color added which is an extract from the annatto seed, a vegetable source.

MARGARINE

W hen margarine was invented in 1870 by the Frenchman Hippolyte Meg–Mouries, it was made by churning ox fat with cream. Today margarine is made from several blends of fats and oils, liquids (water/and or milk), emulsifiers, preservatives, artificial flavors and colors, vitamins, and salt. Each one of these ingredients can be kosher or non-kosher. In Europe, in recent years, three of the six most common blends of fats included whale oil or – animal fat (which, of course is not kosher), and the other three blends often contain some animal fat. (Source: Magnus Pyke, Food Science-and-Technology. Pyke's table – 20 reads as follows:

Six Blends of Fats for Margarine Manufacture

	Percent		Percent
Coconut oil	50-60	Palm kernel oil	50
Hydrogenated		Hydrogenated palm oil	20
Vegetable fat	20-25		
Oil*	20-25	Oil	30
Hydrogenated		Hydrogenated	
groundnut oil	70	whale oil	25
Coconut oil	10	Coconut oil	50
Oil	20	Oil	25
Hydrogenated		Beef fat	25
whale oil	20		
Palm oil	15	Coconut oil	35
Coconut oil	20	Oil	40
Palm kernel oil	20		
Oil	20		

*This can include clarified animal oils from which the solid stearins have been separated of vegetable oil.

Since 1979, almost all American margarines have been made from vegetable oils, but beef-fat margarines are still sold. The difference between hard, soft, and liquid margarine depends on the ratio of fats (solids) to oils (liquids). Maintaining the fats and liquids in solution, rather than in layers, requires emulsifiers, which might be of either animal or vegetable origin. Fats and oils, which by law must constitute 80 percent of margarine, must be meticulously checked to verify their origin and to make sure that the equipment on which they were processed was not used to process animal fats and oils. Absolute stringency is required by Jewish law.

The preservatives, colors, and flavors also require supervision, as explained elsewhere.

The consumer must also be aware that most margarines contain milk or other dairy products. In general, even kosher margarine cannot be assumed to be pareve unless this is specifically stated on the label.

MARSHMALLOWS
(and other gelatin-based foods)

F or over thirty years "Kosher gelatin" has been a substance that the kosher consumer could use as a yardstick to tell if a product was certified by a high or low kosher standard. Up until mid 1993 it was a given that if a product listed "Kosher gelatin" in its ingredients, it meant that the gelatin was definitely derived from non-kosher animals. This was true of all kosher gelatin in the United States, Israel, England, and S. Africa. This was true even when the gelatin was certified kosher by a Rabbi or Rabbinical organization. Those kosher certifiers that adhere to a higher kashrus level, such as the O/U and Star K, categorically rejected the kosher gelatin that was being produced. Instead, these agencies certified various seaweed derivatives, such as insinglass, Irish moss, Spanish moss, agar agar etc. These substances served served as a substitute for real gelatin. Due to the superior gelling qualities of gelatin, a method of producing noncontroversial gelatin was sought. In March of 1993, under the supervision of Rabbi Shimon Eider, "kolatin", a gelatin produced from glatt kosher hides, was finally produced.

Two main questions are asked in connection with gelatin. One, must it come from a kosher source? The second question is: even when it is derived from glatt kosher hides, why isn't it fleishig? The following is a brief description of the five steps involved in making pareve, kosher gelatin.

1. The hide is chemically decomposed and rendered "Nifsal Meachila". In other words, unfit to eat.

2. Although it was considered unfit to eat, people, nevertheless, use it in food. This is called "Achshevay" and reinstitutes gelatin into a food category.

3. Although gelatin is being used as a food, since it is not eaten by itself, but rather mixed in with many other ingredients, it is not fleishig.

4. Even though gelatin is only one ingredient of many, we must bear in mind that it is a very important ingredient and has the status of a "maamid". This means that it is considered a food stabilizer.

5. In conclusion, Reb Moshe Feinstein Zt"l and Rav Aharon Kotler Zt"l, say that gelatin is "taam kalush" (a weak flavor), and is not fleishig, due to the major change it has undergone. However, it must be derived from kosher sources. If the gelatin was derived from a non-kosher source, such as pig or non-kosher slaughtered hides, although they have been chemically altered, since they originated from a non-kosher source, there is no way to ever render them permissible.

SNACKS

O ne of the most frightening dilemmas to face the average parent is "What do I pack for my child's lunch?" In the often intense competition of our children's attention to their products, food companies have gone to great lengths to certify their snack products as kosher. One large company, Post, has gone so far as to distribute a color brochure featuring their products and their appropriate *Brochos*. Equally confusing can be the problem of finding properly certified products for a birthday party. Fortunately, most major companies have now put many of their products under reliable certifications. Raw nuts, dried fruit and raisins without oil, can be used even without certification.

VITAMINS

V itamins require supervision. Common problems: are stearates, gelatin, resinous glazes, meat, (liver extracts and bone meal), fish oil, and glycerine. If vitamins are medically prescribed, a rabbi should be consulted. Following is a listing of natural vitamins and their sources:

VITAMIN D
Function: To enhance intestinal absorption of calcium and phosphorus.
Deficiency: Osteomalacia (softening of the bones in adults), rickets in children.
Sources: Sunshine, fish, liver, egg yolk, milk (most milk today is fortified with Vitamin D).

VITAMIN C
Function: Cellular respiration. Formation of collagen and other fibrous tissue. Metabolism of amino acids.
Deficiency: Scurvy, hemorrhaging, delayed healing, swelling, inflammation of the gums, emaciation, and swollen joints.
Sources: Citrus fruits, strawberries, cantaloupe, kale, brussel sprouts, cabbage, lettuce, tomatoes, potatoes and bean sprouts.

NIACIN (B3)
Function: Assists in cellular respiration. Increases blood flow.
Deficiency: Pellagra, dermatitis, diarrhea, dementia.
Sources: Organ meats, fish, yeast, whole grains, dried peas, beans and nuts.

FOLATE
Function: Necessary for the synthesis of essential nucleic acids, DNA, RNA.
Deficiency: Possibly anemia and a decrease of blood platelets and white cells in the blood. Can cause drowsiness, indigestion, numbness in hands and feet, inflamed tongue.
Natural sources: Organ meats, dark green leafy vegetables, asparagus, lima, beans, yeast, whole grains, wheat germ, lentils, orange juice.

COBALAMIN (B12)
Function: Essential participant in nucleic acid synthesis, and is essential to the structure and function of the nervous system.
Deficiency: Can increase susceptibility to infections.
Sources: Organ meats, fish, milk.

BIOTIN
Function: Synthesis of protein and fatty acids and for the metabolism of carbohydrates.
Deficiency: Can cause severe dermatitis, inflamed and sore tongue, loss of appetite, nausea, depression, anemia, sensitivity of the skin, insomnia and increased blood levels of cholesterol.
Sources: Liver, egg yolk, peanuts, filberts, mushrooms, and cauliflower.

RIBOFLAVIN (B2)
Function: Cellular respiration, also metabolism of Vitamin C.
Deficiency: Over-consumption of carbohydrates.
Sources: Organ meats, fish, dairy products, eggs, green leafy vegetables, whole grains, legumes.

THIAMINE (B1)

Function: Part of the co-enzyme system that makes possible the carbohydrate metabolism.

Deficiency: Beriberi

Sources: Liver, heart, kidneys, yeast, lean meat, green leafy vegetables, whole grain cereals, nuts, berries and legumes.

PYRIDOXINE (B6)

Function: Co-enzyme for many biochemical reactions involving amino acids, helps menstrual regularity, premenstrual tension and acne. May help prevent heart attacks and birth defects.

Deficiency: Greasy, scaling dermatitis around eyes, ears, nose and mouth.

Sources: Liver, whole grain cereals, wheat germ, soybeans, yeast, peanuts, corn, blackstrap molasses.

VITAMIN A (RETINOL)

A. Important in eyes adjusting to darkness. Visual purple, the pigment in the retina for adjusting to darkness needs Vitamin A always.

B. Fights off infection.

C. Skin problems.

Sources of Vitamin A:

A. Pro Vit A (Carotene) is in yellow and orange pigments of many fruits and vegetables.

B. Preformed Vitamin A from animal sources from liver.

C. Can come from egg yolk, green leafy vegetables, deep yellow vegetables.

D. Some Vitamin A natural supplements are from fish liver oil.

WINES AND LIQUORS

At most parties and "simchas" today, we find many people enhancing their level of celebration with the help of some form of alcoholic beverage. Indeed, a well chosen bottle of wine or liqueur makes a perfect gift for almost any occasion. And what better identifies a kiddush in any shul or Jewish home worldwide than the familiar bottles of fine whiskeys and liqueurs on the table? The joyous cry of "Lechayim" has been passed down from one Jewish generation to the next and is still heard today at simchas. Yes, alcoholic beverages play an important part of our lives as Jews. No less important is the knowledge that the kosher consumer must have today regarding the kosher status of the many hundreds of available alcoholic beverages on the market. As with most edible products on the market, alcoholic beverages can have their share of headaches for the kosher consumer. For instance, vermouth, sangria, champagne, sherry brandy and cognac, as well as some liqueurs and cordials, all require supervision because they are wine-based or may contain wine as an ingredient. Needless to say, all wines must have careful supervision. These concerns extend to grape juice and vinegar as well.

Wines

There are few edibles which have the particular status of a truly social food. One class of delicacies, though, is universally considered classy, even though they may be inexpensive and simple: wines. For thousands of years, people have recognized the special "something" which makes wine the drink of toast, of friendship and of love.

It is small wonder, then, that the Torah consistently makes reference to the importance of wine and that the Talmudic rabbis saw fit to establish a special law with regard to wine.

Needless to say, the vast majority of wines on the market today are unfit for consumption by observant Jews.

Strict kashrus supervision is required throughout all stages of the wine-manufacturing process until final bottling.

An interesting prohibition concerning wines relates to the status of boiled wine. Kosher wine that has been cooked before any contact with a non-Jew is exempted from the injunction. Boiled wine is considered "improper" to be offered as a libation to an idol: therefore, if a non-Jew subsequently came into contact with boiled wine, the wine is still permissible to drink. Many kosher wines today bear markings to indicate that they have been boiled. In such a case, it will state on the label "Yayin Mevushal" (boiled wine). Extra caution should be taken with a kosher wine that has not been previously boiled, lest a non-Jew or Jew who is not Shomer Shabbos should come in contact with the bottle of wine (maid etc.)

This winemaking process, from grape to wine glass, yields what may be the most simple and, at the same time, most complex liquid in existence. Simple, because in its most basic state, it is nothing more than fermented grape juice. Complex, because its nuances are boundless, given the countless variables of grape types, processing and aging. The basic ingredient is the grape, which consists of water, sugar, acid and tannin.

The wine industry in Israel was greatly enhanced in 1906 when Baron Edmond de Rothschild gave two vineyards and wineries to the Israeli government. One was in Richon LeZion, near Tel Aviv. The other location was Zichron Yaakov, near Haifa. Several species of grape vines were added from Europe as well as the Reisling grape variety from Germany. Most types of grapes that are used in kosher wines today are carignam, grenache and semillon. Today, the vineyards in Israel consist of almost 40,000 acres, and produce over 13 million gallons of wines per year. Currently kosher wines are being produced in such places as Spain, Italy, New York, California, Israel, and Italy, among others.

This is a brief description of how wine is made:

Preparation - The grapes are crushed and destemmed in a machine, then poured into a wood, steel, cement or fiberglass fermentation vat. For white wine, the skins usually are removed immediately after crushing. Sulphur dioxide as an antiseptic may be added before fermentation.

Fermentation - Natural yeasts start the fermentation when the temperature exceeds 65 degrees, but cultured yeasts, developed to suit a certain grape or wine style, are added to speed and control the process. In red wines, the grape mixture is heated, usually to about 75 degrees. In most white wines, a cooler fermentation is preferred. When the sugar is almost completely converted to alcohol, the fermentation ends.

During fermentation, sugar or sterilized grape juice may be injected for sweetness, acids for tartness, and certain flavorings, like oak shavings, may be added to provide extra tannin.

Maturation - Most red wine is filtered, then aged from a few months to 3 years. The better reds draw complex flavors from oak barrels. White wines generally are stored briefly and away from air in concrete or cement tanks. During maturation, the wine is filtered and clarified, often employing several additives.

Bottling - Most white wines are bottled within 9 months after harvest, while red wines are bottled between 2 and 10 years after picking. Wines continue to age in the bottle, with acid and tannin softening over time. Fine red wines may continue to improve for 30 years or longer.

Wine Facts: As of the date of this second edition, of special interest to wine consumers may be some of the following facts:

a.) **KEDEM** 1 1/2 Litre bottles of wine are **NOT** Mevushal.

b.) **KEDEM** Domestic 187 ml. and 750 ml. bottles of wine are **ALWAYS** Mevushal.

c.) In **KEDEM'S** 3 Litre bottles, only the Burgandy, Chablois & Sherry **ARE** Mevushal.

d.) **KEDEM** Baron Herzog are **ALL** Mevushal except for those marked "Special Reserve", which are **NOT** Mevushal.

e.) **ALL MANISCHEWITZ** wines are Mevushal.

f.) All O/U Grape Juices are Mevushal.

g.) **TIROSH** wines in the 75 ml. bottles **are** Mevushal.

h.) **TIROSH** wines in the 1500 ml. bottles, are **NOT** Mevushal.

i .) **WEINSTOCK** wines are **ALL** Mevushal. All **ASHALON** Wines are not Mevushal, all **GOLAN** Wines are not Mevushal except for Sauvignon Blanc. All **GAMLA** Wines are not Mevushal except Sauvignon Blanc and Red Emerald Hill.

Liqueurs

Liqueurs are generally made by adding flavoring to high proof distilled spirit. A liqueur can contain many ingredients of concern to the kosher consumer. The first ingredient to check is the alcohol base itself. This is sometimes a grape alcohol from the surplus grape crop. Another important concern is the flavoring of the liqueur. Chartreuse liqueur has over 130 herbs, peels, roots and spices all contributing to is flavor. Most liqueurs fall into 4 main categories. a.) fruit liqueur b.) citrus liqueur c.) herb liqueur d.) bean and kernel liqueur.

In fruit brandy, for instance, **CREME DE CASSIS** is made near Dijon, France from black currants and grape brandy. Without proper supervision, this would be prohibited to the kosher consumer.

Among the citrus liqueurs is **COINTREAU**, which is a Triple-Sec Curacao. This and **GRAND MARNIER**, from the Bordeaux wine region, have a champagne Cognac base, and are not kosher.

TIA MARIA liqueur is an example of a bean and kernel liqueur. It is produced by the use of blue mountain coffee extract in Jamaican cane spirit. **KAHLUA** is made in a similar fashion in Mexico. **DRAMBUIE**, which in Gaelic means "Drink that satisfies", is made from a base of single-malt scotch whiskey with added beaten honey and herbs. All of the above liqueurs are recommended.

Since the essence of a liqueur is in its flavor, many are shrouded in secrecy. **BENEDICTINE**, for instance, is made by a company founded in

1863 in Normandy. Among its ingredients are: cinnamon, cardomom, bitter aloes, nutmeg, saffron, musk seeds, myrrh, angelica seeds, mace and 17 other ingredients.

Vermouth is always wine based, hence a good certification is always needed.

Whiskeys

Scotch whiskey has been around for close to 500 years. Although some companies still produce single malt whiskey (e.g. **GLENLIVET**), most blend from 15 to 50 different malts to achieve the flavor they desire. The malt is made from barley, and later combined with a mostly tasteless grain alcohol base. **CHIVAS REGAL**, for instance, uses over 30 malt whiskeys in their product. U.S. produced whiskey is usually made either from rye, corn or barley. These are often blended. It is important to note that the U.S. government allows up to 2.5% sherry (wine based) to be added to the whiskey blend. This can cause problems for the kosher consumer. **Canadian whiskey** is rye and barley. It is then aged in used American bourbon barrels. **SEAGRAM'S V.O.** whiskey, one of the most popular, is a blend of over 120 different whiskeys.

Mescal & Tequila

Mescal, and its cousin tequila, are made by the following process: *Agave* plants which are about to flower (the terminal event in the life of the plant) are cut off at the roots, their leaves removed, leaving a globular stem called a "cabeza" (Spanish for head). The cabeza is then baked, to convert the starches and polysaccharides (which build up in the stem in anticipation of flowering) into sugars. The cabeza is shredded, and the liquid extracted. This liquid is fermented and then distilled into mescal. Commercial mescal and tequila are generally distilled twice, to 110 proof, then watered back down to 80 proof.

The difference between mescal and tequila is the place in which it is made. Much like the wines of Bordeaux, tequila comes from the Tequila region of the state of Jalisco, Mexico. (Only one cultivar, the Aqul: (Spanish for blue) variety of *Agave Tequilana,* called blue maguey, is cultivated there.)

The distilled product from other species of *Agave,* or from outside the Tequila region, is generally called mescal. Some are known by local names. A good deal of it is bootlegged.

The larvae which are put in some bottles of tequilla are natural parasites who feed on the rich stem and root tissues of *Agave* plants. Why is this misnamed "worm" added? It is an indication of the proof of the liquor. If the larva is in good shape, it means that the percentage of alcohol is high enough to keep it preserved. However, if the booze has been watered down, the larva goes bad. Although most tequilla is acceptable, those with the worm inside of course are not.

A FEW WORDS ABOUT INSECTS IN YOUR FOOD

Although eating insects is strictly forbidden by the Torah, we find this concern often overlooked. Following is an example of some products that may contain bugs or worms.

It is important to realize that we are prohibited from the Torah (Vayikra XI) to eat Sheratzim. This issue includes many types of insects. Therefore, a bowl of salad which may look kosher, could have more non-kosher ingredients (bugs) and prohibitions than a cheeseburger at a local fast food restaurant. Although Reb Moshe Feinstein zt"l states that it is not mandatory at this time to check vegetables for bugs, he was refering to a time when DDT (a strong pesticide) was widely used on most crops. This pesticide, when used, served to temporarily eliminate the vast majority of insects from vegetables. Unfortunately, due to various agricultural modifications, the insects are back! In the United States, the insecticide DDT is now officially and legally outlawed. Now, often over half a dozen species can be found on one head of lettuce. Usually, something as small as an insect would be "batel" (anulled) in a large volume of permissible food. In the case of insects, however, this is not the case. The reason is that we have a rule which states that a complete creature cannot become nullified. Therefore, a worm on the bottom of a tequilla bottle does not become nullified by the liquid. However, if a person cooked soup and found a fly floating in it later, the fly should be removed and the soup will now be permissible. If there were three or more insects in the food, we have to assume that it was infested with insects and must be sifted, strained etc. If there are only parts of insects, they are considered nullified in sixty. However, whenever possible, a person must try to remove the insect parts as well. This is the reason why in Israel many people who have found insecdt parts in their flour always sift it. In most countries, flour is pre-sifted. Microscopic insect parts do not concern us halachically. The following FDA list shows the maximum givernment tolerance when it comes to insects found in food, and illustrates clearly how we often are not aware of what we are eating. There is a company in Israel that grows their produce in sand, which has proved effective in avoiding insect infestation even in leafy vegetable. In the U.S., pre-checked lettuce, cabbage etc. are being marketed under a reliable hecher. The chart on page 195 will explain how to check for bugs in most cases.

Chitin

Chitin, a chemical derived from the shells of lobsters, crabs, and crayfish (and potentially from insects) has been approved for use in cereals by the Japanese as a source of fiber and calcium. This has not affected the produce in the U.S. at this time.

DO YOU KNOW WHAT YOU ARE EATING??

The process by which ingredients are produced must be carefully checked. In fact, it is necessary to check the processing locations to verify that hygienic standards are not so lax as to allow insects or worms to contaminate the food product. Unfortunately, lax hygiene in food processing is more common than people wish to believe.

The food defect action levels contained in this list are set on the basis of no hazard to health. Any products that might be harmful to consumers are acted against on the basis of their hazard to health, whether or not they exceed the action levels. In addition, poor manufacturing practices will result in regulatory actions, whether the product is above or below the defect action level. The defect action levels are set because it is not possible, and never has been possible, to grow in open fields, harvest, and process crops that are totally free of natural defects.

Department of Health and Human Services
Public Health Service
Food and Drug Administration
Center for Food Safety and Applied Nutrition
Washington, DC 20204

PRODUCT	DEFECT (Method)	ACTION LEVEL
ALLSPICE	Mold (MPM-V32)	Average of 5% or more berries by weight are moldy
APPLE BUTTER	Mold (AOAC 44.197)	Average of mold count is 12% or more
	Rodent filth (AOAC 44.086)	Average of 4 or more rodent hairs per 100 grams of apple butter
	Insects (AOAC 44.086)	Average of 5 or more whole or equivalent insects (not counting mites, aphids, thrips, or scale insects) per 100 grams of apple butter

PRODUCT	DEFECT (Method)	ACTION LEVEL
APRICOT, PEACH, AND PEAR NECTARS AND PUREES	Mold (AOAC 44.202)	Average mold count is 12% or more
APRICOTS, CANNED	Insect filth (MPM -V51)	Average of 2% or more by count insect-infested or insect-damaged in a minimum of 10 subsamples.
ASPARAGUS, CANNED	Insect filth (MPM-V93)	10% by count of spears or pieces are infested with 6 or more attached asparagus beetle eggs and/or sacs
	Insects (MPM-V93)	Asparagus contains an average of 40 or more thrips per 100 grams OR
		Insects (whole or equivalent) of any size average 5 or more per 100 grams OR
		Insects (whole or equivalent) of 3mm or longer have an average aggregate length of 7mm or longer per 100 grams of asparagus
BAY (LAUREL) LEAVES	Mold (MPH-V32)	Average of 5% or more of pieces by weight are moldy
		Average of 5% or more pieces by weight are insect-infested
	Mammalian Excreta	Average of 1 mg or more mammalian excreta per pound after processing
BEETS,	Rot will dry rot	Average of 5% or more pieces by weight CANNED
BERRIES Drupelet, Canned and Frozen (blackberries, raspberries, etc.)	Mold (AOAC 44.205)	Average mold count is 60% or more
	Insects and larvae (AOAC 44.089)	Average of 4 or more larvae per 500 grams OR
		Average of 10 or more whole insects or equivalent per 500 grams (excluding thrips, aphids and mites)

PRODUCT	DEFECT (Method)	ACTION LEVEL
Ligon, Canned	Insect larvae (MPM-V64)	Average of 3 or more larvae per pound in a minimum of 12 subsamples
Multer, Canned	Insects (MPM-V64)	Average of 40 or more thrips per No. 2 can in all subsamples and 20% of subsamples are materially infested
BROCCOLI,	Insects and (AOAC 44.108)	Average of 60 or more aphids, thrips and/FROZEN or mites per 100 grams
CAPSICUM: Pods	Insect filth and/or mold (MPM-V32)	Average of more than 3% of pods by weight are insect-infested and/or moldy
Ground Capsicum (excluding paprika)	Mold (AOAC 44.213)	Average mold count is more than 20%
	Insect filth (AOAC 44.131)	Average of more than 50 insect fragments per 25 grams
	Rodent filth (AOAC 44.131)	Average of more than 6 rodent hairs per 25 grams
Ground Paprika	Mold (AOAC 44.213)	Average mold count is more than 20%
	Insect filth (AOAC 44.146)	Average of more than 75 insect fragments per 25 grams
	Rodent filth (AOAC 44.146)	Average of more than 11 rodent hairs per 25 grams
CASSIA OR MON BARK (WHOLE)	Mold (MPM-V32)	Average of 5% or more pieces by weight CINNA- are moldy
	Insect filth (MPM-V32)	Average of 5% or more pieces by weight are insect-infested
	Mammalian (MPM-V32)	Average of more than 1 mg or more mammalian excreta per pound
CHERRIES Brined and Maraschino	Insect filth (MPM-V48)	Average of 5% or more pieces are rejects due to maggots

PRODUCT	DEFECT (Method)	ACTION LEVEL
Fresh, Canned or Frozen	Rot (MPM-V48)	Average of 7% or more pieces are rejects due to rot
	Insect filth (MPM-V48)	Average of 4% or more pieces are rejects due to insects other than maggots
CHERRY JAM	Mold (MPM-V61)	Average mold count is 30% or more
CHOCOLATE & CHOCOLATE LIQUOR	Insect filth (AOAC 44.007)	Average is 60 or more microscopic insect fragments per 100 grams
		Any 1 subsample contains 90 or more insect fragments
	Rodent filth (AOAC 44.007)	Average is more than 1 rodent hair per 100 grams in 6 100-gram subsamples examined OR
	Shell (AOAC 44.012-13.026)	For chocolate liquor, if the shell is in excess of 2% calculated on the basis of alkali-free nibs
	Insects & insect eggs (AOAC 44.095 & 44.096)	5 or more Drosophila and other fly eggs per 250 ml or 1 or more
CLOVES	Stems (MPM-V32)	Average of 5% or more stems by weight
COCOA BEANS	Mold (MPM-V18)	More than 4% of beans by count are moldy
	Insect filth (MPM-V18)	More than 4% of beans by count are insect-infested including insect-damaged
	Insect filth and/or mold (MPM-V18)	More than 6% of beans by count are insect-infested or moldy
	Mammalian excreta(MPM-V18)	Mammalian excreta is 10 mg per pound or more
COCOA POWDER PRESS CAKE	Insect filth (AOAC 44.007)	Average of 75 or more microscopic insect fragments per subsample of 50 grams

PRODUCT	DEFECT (Method)	ACTION LEVEL
		Any 1 subsample contains 125 or more microscopic insect fragments
	Rodent filth (AOAC 44.007)	Average in 6 or more subsamples is more than 2 rodent hairs per subsample of 50 grams OR
		Any 1 subsample contains more than 4 rodent hairs
	Shell (AOAC 44.13.012-13.026)	2% or more shell calculated on the basis of alkali-free nibs
COFFEE BEANS,	Insect filth & insects (MPM-V1)	Average 10% or more by count are insect-infested or insect-damaged OR
		If live insect infestation is present, 1 live insect in each of 2 or more immediate containers, or 1 dead insect in each of 3 or more immediate containers, or 3 live or dead insects in 1 immediate container AND
		Similar live or dead insect infestation present on or in immediate proximity of the lot OR
		1 or more live insects in each of 3 or more immediate containers OR
		2 or more dead whole insects in 5 or more immediate containers OR
		2 or more live or dead insects on 5 or more of cloth or burlap containers
	Mold (MPM-V1)	Average of 10% or more beans by count are moldy
COFFEE BEANS, GRADED GREEN	Poor Grade	Beans are poorer than Grade 8 of the New York Green Coffee Association
CONDIMENTAL SEEDS OTHER THAN FENNEL SEEDS AND SESAME SEEDS	Mammalian (MPM-V32)	Average of 3 mg or more of mammalian excreta per pound

PRODUCT	DEFECT (Method)	ACTION LEVEL
CORN: SWEET CORN, CANNED CANNED	Insect larvae ear worms, corn borers) (AOAC 44.109)	2 or more 3mm or longer larvae, cast skins, larval or cast skin fragments of corn ear worm or corn borer and the aggregate length of such larvae, cast skins, larval or cast skin fragments exceeds 12mm in 24 pounds (24 No. 303 cans or equivalent)
CORN HUSKS FOR TAMALES	Insect filth (MPM-V115)	Average of 5% or more pieces by weight of the corn husks examine insect-infested (including insect-damaged)
	Mold (MPM-V115)	Average of 5% or more pieces by weight are moldy
CORNMEAL	Insects	Average of 1 or more whole insect (or equivalent) per 500 grams
	Insect filth (AOAC 048)	Average of 25 or more insect fragments per 25 grams
	Rodent filth (AOAC 048)	Average of 1 or more rodent hairs per 25 grams OR

Average of 1 or more rodent excreta fragment per 50 grams |
| CRANBERRY SAUCE | Mold (AOAC 44.200) | Average mold count is more than 15% OE

The mold count of any 1 subsample is more than 50% |
CUMIN SEED	Sand and grit (AOAC 44.124)	Average of 9.5% or more ash and/or 1.5% or more acid insoluble ash
CURRANT JAM BLACK	Mold (MPM-V61)	Average mold count is 75% or more
CURRANTS	Insect filth	5% or more by count wormy in the average of the subsamples
CURRY POWDER	Insect filth (AOAC 44.124)	Average of 100 or more insect fragments per 25 grams
	Rodent filth (AOAC 44.124)	Average of 4 or more rodent hairs per 25 grams

PRODUCT	DEFECT (Method)	ACTION LEVEL
DATE MATERIAL (CHOPPED, SLICED, OR MACERATED)	Insects (MPM-V53)	10 or more dead insects in 1 or more subsamples OR 5 or more dead insects (whole or equivalent) per 100 grams
	Pits (MPM-V53)	2 or more pits and/or pit fragments 2 mm or longer measured in the longest dimension per 900 grams
DATES, PITTED	Multiple (MPM-V53)	Average of 5% or more dates by count are rejects (moldy, dead insects, insect excreta, sour, dirty, and/or worthless) as determined by macroscopic sequential examination
	Pits (MPM-V53)	Average of 2 or more pits and/or pit fragments 2 mm or longer in the longest dimension per 100 dates
DATES, WHOLE	Multiple (MPM-V53)	Average of 5% or more dates by count are rejects (moldy, dead insects, insect excreta, sour, dirty, and/or worthless) as determined by macroscopic sequential examination
EGGS & OTHER EGG PRODUCTS, FROZEN	Decomposition (AOAC 46.003-46.012)	2 or more cans decomposed and at least 2 subsamples from decomposed cans have direct microscopic counts of 5 million or more bacteria per gram
FENNEL SEED	Insects (MPM-V32)	20% or more of subsamples contain insects
	Mammalian (MPM-V32)	20% mor more of subsamples contain mammalian excreta OR Average of 3 mg or more of mammalian excreta per pound
FIG PASTE	Insects (AOAC 44.092 44.093)	Over 13 insect heads per 100 grams of fig paste in each of 2 or more subsamples

PRODUCT	DEFECT (Method)	ACTION LEVEL
FIGS	Insect filth &/or mold &/or dirty fruit or pieces of fruit (MPM-V53)	Average of 10% or more pieces by count are rejects Average of more than 10% of pieces are insect-infested &/or moldy dirty fruit or pieces of fruit
FISH, FRESH OR FROZEN (APPLIES TO FISH OR FILLETS WEIGHING 3 POUNDS OR LESS)	Decomposition	Decomposition in 5% or more of the fish fillets in the sample (but not less than 5) show Class 3 decomposition over at least 25% of their areas OR 20% or more of the fish or fillets in the sample (but not less than 5) showing Class 3 decomposition over at least 25% of their areas OR The percentage of fish or fillets showing Class 2 decomposition as above plus 4 times the percentage of those showing Class 3 decomposition as above equals at least 20% and there are at least 5 decomposed fish or fillets in the sample

Classes of Decomposition: 1). No odor or decomposition 2) Slight odor of decomposition 3) Definite odor of decomposition

Tullibees, Ciscoes, Inconnus, Chubs & Whitefish	Parasites (cysts) (MPM-V28)	50 parasitic cysts per 100 pounds (whole or fillets,) provided that 20% of the fish examined are infested
Blue Fin & other Fresh Water Herring	Parasites (cysts) (MPM-V28)	60 cysts per 100 fish (fish averaging 1 pound or less) or 100 pounds of fish (fish averaging over 1 pound,) provided that 20% of the fish examined are infested
Red Fish & Ocean Perch	Parasites (copepods) (MPM-V28)	3% of the fillets examined contain 1 or more copepods accompanied by pus pockets
GINGER, WHOLE	Insect filth &/or mold (MPM-V32)	Average of 3% or more pieces by weight are insect-infested and/or moldy
	Mammalian excreta (MPM-V32)	Average of 3 mg or more of mammalian excreta per pound

PRODUCT	DEFECT (Method)	ACTION LEVEL
GREENS,	Mildew	Average of 10% or more of leaves, by count or weight, showing mildew over 1/2" in diameter
HOPS	Insects (aphids) (AOAC 44.009)	Average of more than 2,500 aphids per 10 grams
MACARONI & NOODLE PRODUCTS	Insect filth (AOAC 44.069)	Average of insect fragments equal or exceeds 225 per 225 grams in 6 or more subsamples
	Rodent filth (AOAC 44.069)	Average of rodent hairs equals or exceeds 4.5 per 225 grams in 6 or more subsamples
MACE	Insect filth &/or mold (MPM-V32)	Average of 3% or more pieces by weight and insect-infested &/or moldy
	Mammalian excreta (MPM-V32)	Average of 3 mg or more of mammalian excreta per pound
	Foreign matter (MPM-V32)	Average of 1.5% or more of foreign matter through a 20-mesh sieve
MUSHROOMS CANNED & DRIED	Insects (AOAC 44.115 & 44.116)	Average of 20 or more maggots of any size per 100 grams of drained mushrooms and proportionate liquid or 15 grams of dried mushrooms OR
		Average of 5 or more maggots 2 mm or longer per 100 grams of drained mushrooms and proportionate liquid or 15 grams of dried mushrooms
	Mites (AOAC 44.115 & 44.116)	Average of 75 mites per 100 grams drained mushrooms and proportionate liquid or 15 grams of dried mushrooms
	Decomposition (MPM-V100)	Average of more than 10%, by weight, of mushrooms are decomposed
NUTMEG	Insect filth &/or	Average of 10% or more pieces by count are insect-infested &/or moldy

PRODUCT	DEFECT (Method)	ACTION LEVEL	
NUTS, TREE	Multiple defects (MPM-V81)	Reject nuts (insect-infested, rancid, moldy, gummy, and shriveled or empty shells) as determined by macroscopic examination at or in excess of the following levels	
		Unshelled %	Shelled %
Almonds		5	5
Brazils		10	5
Cashew		---	5
Green Chestnuts		5	----
Baked Chestnut		10	----
Dried Chestnuts		----	5
Filberts		10	5
Lichee Nuts		15	----
Pecans		10	5
Pili Nuts		15	10
Pistachios		10	5
Walnuts		10	5

OLIVES:

Product	Defect (Method)	Action Level
Pitted	Pits (MPM-V67)	Average of 1.3 or more by count of olives with whole pits and/or pit fragments 2 mm or longer measured in the longest dimension
Imported Greens	Insect damage (MPM-V67)	7% or more by count showing damage by olive fruit fly
Salad	Pits (MPM-V67)	Average of 1.3 or more by count of olives with whole pits and/or pit fragments 2 mm
	(MPM-V67)	9% or more by count showing damage by olive fruit fly
Salt-cured	Insects (MPM-V71)	Average of 6 subsamples is 10% or more olives by count with 10 or more scale insects each
	Mold (MPM-V67)	Average of 6 subsamples is 25% or more olives by count are moldy
Imported	Insect damage (MPM-V67)	10% or more by count showing damage by olive fruit fly
PEACHES, CANNED & FROZEN	Moldy or Wormy (MPM-V51)	Average of 3% or more fruit by count are wormy or moldy

PRODUCT	DEFECT (Method)	ACTION LEVEL
	Insect damage (MPM-V51)	In 12 -pound cans or equivalent, one or more larvae and/or larval fragments whose aggregate length exceeds 5 mm
PEANUT BUTTER	Insect filth (AOAC 44.037)	Average of 30 or more insect fragments per 100 grams
	Rodent filth (AOAC 44.0354	Average of 1 or more rodent hairs per 100 grams
	Grit (AOAC 44.034)	Gritty taste and water insoluble inorganic residue is more than 25 mg per 100 grams
PEANUTS, SHELLED	Multiple defects (MPM-V89)	Average of 5% or more kernels by count are rejects (insect-infested, moldy, rancid, otherwise decomposed, blanks, and shriveled)
	Insects (MPM-V89)	Average of 20 or more whole insects or equivalent in 100-pound bag siftings
PEANUTS, UNSHELLED	Multiple defects (MPM-V89)	Average of 10% or more peanuts by count are rejects (insect-infested, moldy, rancid, otherwise decomposed, blanks, and shriveled)
PEAS: BLACK-EYE COWPEAS, FIELDPEAS, DRIED	Insect damage (MPM-V104)	Average of 10% or more by count of class 6 damage or higher in minimum of 12 subsamples.
PEAS: COWPEAS BLACK-EYE PEAS (SUCCULENT,) CANNED	Insect larvae (MPM-V104)	Average of 5 or more cowpea curculio larvae or the equivalent per No. 2 can
PEAS & BEANS, DRIED	Insect filth (MPM-V104)	Average of 5% or more by count insect-infested and/or insect-damaged by storage insects in minimum of 12 subsamples.
PEPPER, WHOLE	Insect filth &/or mold (MPM-V39)	Average of 1% or more pieces by weight are insect-infested and/or moldy
	Mammalian excreta (MPM-V39)	Average of 1% or more mammalian excreta per pound
	Foreign matter (MPM-V39)	Average of 1% or more pickings and siftings by weight

PRODUCT	DEFECT (Method)	ACTION LEVEL
PINEAPPLE, CANNED	Mold	Average mold count for 6 subsamples is (AOAC 44.199) 20% or more OR the mold count of any 1 subsample is 60% or more
PINEAPPLE JUICE	Mold (AOAC 44.199)	Average mold count for 6 subsamples is 15% or more OR The mold count of any 1 subsample is 40% or more
PLUMS, CANNED	Rot (MPM-V51)	Average of 5% or more plums by count with rot spots larger than the area of a circle 12 mm in diameter
POPCORN	Rodent filth (AOAC 44.099)	1 or more rodent excreta pellets are found in 1 or more subsamples, and 1 or more rodent hairs are found in 2 or more other subsamples OR 2 or more rodent hairs per pound and rodent hair is found in 50% or more of the subsamples OR
	Field corn	5% or more by weight of field corn
POTATO CHIPS	Rot (MPM-V113)	Average of 6% or more pieces by weight contain rot
PRUNES: DRIED & DEHYDRATED LOW-MOISTURE	Multiple defects (MPM-V53)	Average of a minimum of 10 subsamples is 5% or more prunes by count are rejects (insect-infested, moldy or decomposed, dirty, and/or otherwise unfit)
PRUNES, PITTED	Pits (MPM-V53)	Average of 10 subsamples is 2% or more by count with whole pits and/or pit fragments 2 mm or longer and 4 or more of 10 subsamples of pitted prunes have 2% or more by count with whole pits and/or pit fragments 2 mm or longer

PRODUCT	DEFECT (Method)	ACTION LEVEL
RAISINS	Mold (MPM-V76)	Average of 10 subsamples is 5% or more raisins by count are moldy
	Sand & Grit (MPM-V76)	Average of 10 subsamples is 40 mg or more of sand and grit per 100 grams of natural or golden bleached raisins
	Insects and Insect eggs (AOAC 44.097 & MPM-V76)	10 or more whole or equivalent insects and 35 Drosophila eggs per 8 oz. of golden bleached raisins
SALMON, CANNED	Decomposition	2 or more Class 3 defective cans, regardless of lot or container size OR

2 to 30 Class 2 and/or Class 3 defective cans as required by sampling plan based on lot size and container size

(A defective can is defined as one that contains Class 2 or Class 3 decomposition –see FISH product listing.) Sampling plan tables are available on request from FDA) |
SESAME SEEDS	Insect filth (MPM-V32)	Average of 5% or more seeds by weight are insect-infested
	Mold (MPM-V32)	Average of 5% or more seeds by weight are decomposed
	Mammalian excreta (MPM-V32)	Average of 5 mg or more mammalian excreta per pound
	Foreign Matter (MPM-V32)	Average of .5% or more foreign matter by weight
SHRIMP: FRESH FROZEN, RAW, HEADLESS PEELED OR BREADED)	Decomposition	5% or more are Class 3 or 20% or more are Class 2 decomposition as determined by organoleptic examination OR

If percentage of Class 2 shrimp plus 4 times percent of Class 3 equals or exceeds 20% (See FISH product listing for definition of decomposition classes) |

217

PRODUCT	**DEFECT** **(Method)**	**ACTION LEVEL**
SHRIMP: IMPORTED CANNED OR COOKED/FROZEN		
	Decomposition	Indole levels in two or more subsamples equal or exceed 25 micrograms per 100 grams for both original and check analysis
SPICES, LEAFY, OTHER THAN BAY LEAVES		
	Insect filth &/or mold (MPM-V32)	Average of 5% or more pieces by weight are insect-infested &/or moldy
	Mammalian excreta (MPM-V32)	Average of 1 mg or more of Mammalian excreta per pound after processing
SPINACH, CANNED OR FROZEN	Insects & Mites (AOAC 44.110)	Average of 50 or more aphids and/or thrips &/or mites per 100 grams OR
		2 or more 3 mm or longer larvae &/or larval fragments of spinach worms (caterpillars) whose aggregate length exceeds 12 mm are present in 24 pounds OR
		Leaf miners of any size average 8 or more per 100 grams or leaf miners 3 mm or longer average 4 or more per 100 grams
STRAWBERRIES: FROZEN WHOLE OR SLICED		
	Mold (AOAC 44.205)	Average mold count of 45% or more and mold count of at least half of the subsamples is 55% or more
	Grit	Berries taste gritty
TOMATOES, CANNED		
	Drosophila fly (AOAC 44.119)	Average of 10 or more fly eggs per 500 grams; or 5 or more fly eggs and 1 or more maggots per 500 grams; or 2 or more maggots per 500 grams, in a minimum of 12 subsamples
TOMATOES, CANNED WITH OR WITHOUT JUICE (BASED ON DRAINED JUICE)	Mold (AOAC 44.206)	Average mold count in 6 subsamples is more than 15% and the mold counts of all of the subsamples are more than 12%

PRODUCT	DEFECT (Method)	ACTION LEVEL
TOMATOES, CANNED (PACKED IN TOMATO PUREE (BASED ON DRAINED LIQUID)	Mold (AOAC 44.206)	Average mold count in 6 subsamples is more than 29% and the counts of all of the subsamples are more than 25%
TOMATO JUICE	Drosophila fly (AOAC 44.119)	Average of 10 or more fly eggs per 100 grams; or 5 or more fly eggs and 2 or more maggots per 100 grams; or 2 or more maggots per 100 grams, in a minimum of 12 subsamples
	Mold (AOAC 44.207)	Average mold count in 6 subsamples is 24% or more and the mold count of all of the subsamples are more than 20%
TOMATO PASTE, PIZZA & OTHER SAUCES	Drosophila fly (AOAC 44.119)	Average of 30 or more fly eggs per 100 grams; or 5 or more fly eggs and 1 or more maggots per 100 grams; or 2 or more maggots per 100 grams, in a minimum of 12 subsamples
TOMATO PUREE	Drosophila fly (AOAC 44.119)	Average of 20 or more fly eggs per 100 grams; or 10 or more fly eggs and 1 or more maggots per 100 grams; or 2 or more maggots per 100 grams, in a minimum of 12 subsamples
TOMATO PASTE OR PUREE	Mold (AOAC 44.207)	Average mold count in 6 subsamples is 45% or more and the mold counts of all of the subsamples are more than 40%
PIZZA AND OTHER SAUCES	Mold (AOAC 44.209)	Average mold count in 6 subsamples is more than 34% and the counts of all of the subsamples are more than 30%
TOMATO SAUCE	Mold (AOAC 44.207)	Average mold count in 6 subsamples is 45% or more and the mold count of all of the subsamples are more than 40%
TOMATO CATSUP	Mold (AOAC 44.207)	Average mold count in 6 subsamples is 55% or more

PRODUCT	DEFECT (Method)	ACTION LEVEL
TOMATO POWDER (EXCEPT SPRAY-DRIED)	Mold (AOAC 44.211)	Average mold count in 6 subsamples is 45% or more and the mold counts of all of the subsamples are more than 40%
TOMATO POWDER SPRAY-DRIED	Mold (A0AC 44.211)	Average mold count in 6 subsamples is 67% or more
TOMATO SOUP & TOMATO PRODUCTS	Mold (AOAC 44.208)	Average mold count in 6 subsamples is 45% or more and the mold counts of all of the subsamples are more than 40%
TUNA, CANNED: ALBACORE, SKIPJACK, AND YELLOWFIN	Histamine	Histamine content per subsample equals or exceeds 20 mg per 100 grams in both original and check analysis (two subsamples minimum)
WHEAT	Insect damage (MPM-V15)	Average of 32 or more insect-damaged kernels per 100 grams
	Rodent filth (MPM-V15)	Average of 9 mg or more rodent excreta pellets and/or pellet fragments per kilogram
WHEAT FLOUR	Insect filth (AOAC 44.052)	Average of 50 or more insect fragments per 500 grams in 6 subsamples
	Rodent filth (AOAC 44.052)	Average of 1 or more rodent hairs per 500 grams in 6 subsamples

VEGETABLE INSPECTION

SPECIFIC INSPECTION GUIDELINES

ARTICHOKE:
Each leaf down to the heart of the plant must be inspected (Rabbi Pinchas Bodner).

ASPARAGUS:
• Canned: Pour liquid into a lightly colored bowl and inspect the liquid from the can for insects. If any insects are found the asparagus may not be used.
• Frozen: Method A.
• Fresh: Treat as florets and follow method E. After this treatment, peel the scales and discard.

BOSTON LETTUCE:
Method B.

BELGIAN ENDIVES:
Method C.

BROCCOLI:
• Florets: Method E.
• Frozen: Method A.
• Stalks: Method D.

BRUSSELS SPROUTS:
(Fresh and Frozen). Not recommended, since the inspection methods are not reliable.[1,2]

CABBAGE:
Shopping tip: Choose a clean head without soft spots and cracked bases. Method C.

CAULIFLOWER:
Cook, preserve or refrigerate immediately after inspecting.
• Florets: Method E.
• Frozen: Method A.
• Stalks: Method D.

CELERY:
• Leaves: procedure for Parsley (For cooking).
• Stalks: Method D.

DILL:
• Dried: Permitted without inspection.
• Fresh, for cooking: Follow procedure for Parsley (for cooking).

ESCAROLE:
Shopping tip: Choose fresh, firm heads. • Method B.

KALE: Method B.

ICEBERG LETTUCE:
Shopping tip: Choose a clean head without soft spots and cracked bases. • Method C.
• After the inspection, it is not advisable to reuse the store's wrapping.

ONIONS:
Shopping tip: Choose firm onions without shoots.
• Peel onion until the second good layer. The remainder of the onion may be used without further inspection.

PARSLEY:
• Flakes: Permitted without inspection.
• Raw: Not recommended.[1]
• For cooking: Treat the parsley sprigs as florets and follow Method E.
Cooking tip: To use as a seasoning when cooking, place parsley in a closed gourmet bag. Discard parsley after cooking.

ROMAINE LETTUCE:
• Leaves: Method B.
• Stalks: Method D.

SPINACH:
• Fresh: Treat as florets and follow Method E.
• Frozen: Method A.

1. Rabbi Shimon Schwab
2. Rabbi Moshe Heinemann
3. Rabbi Shimon Eider

The views of the Poskim cited here are found in their articles on this subject. When a Posek is not cited, this does not necessarily mean that he disagrees with a given approach, but merely that he has not issued a written opinion on this specific issue.

METHODS FOR INSPECTING VEGETABLES

Shopping hint: To avoid as many problems of infestation as possible, always buy U.S. FANCY or U.S. GRADE A vegetables that are clean and crisp.

SHABBOS CAUTION: Because of the Shabbos prohibition of selecting, *Borrer,* whenever an insect is found on a vegetable the insect alone may not be removed. Rather, part of the vegetable containing the insect and an additional portion should be cut away, thereby effectively removing the insect from the vegetable. Any procedures requiring soaking the vegetable in salt water should not be done on Shabbos.

A NOTE ON INSPECTING VEGETABLES:
The surface of the vegetable should be inspected in proper lighting. If the leaf is translucent (e.g., lettuce), backlighting may also be used.

METHODS OF INSPECTION
The following is a summary of the methods suggested recently by some Poskim to properly inspect vegetables. Because there are different opinions regarding the appropriate cleaning and inspection methods, each individual should consult his Rav for a definitive ruling.

METHOD A
Some Poskim hold that frozen vegetables may be used without special inspection. Others hold some appropriate form of inspection is required.[1,2]

METHOD B
Since infestation is so prevalent, only the most rigorous treatment will permit the use of the leaves.

In the spring and summer, *each leaf* must be washed well and carefully inspected on both sides.

In the fall and winter, when infestation is not as prevalent, the leaves should be soaked in a vinegar solution and flushed in water. Three leaves should be randomly selected and then inspected to determine if the soaking procedure did in fact remove all insects. If these three leaves prove to be insect-free, the remaining leaves do not need to be inspected.[3] If, however, even one of these three leaves is contaminated, then all the leaves of the vegetable must be inspected.[3] Others hold that under all circumstances, all the leaves must be visually inspected.[1]

METHOD C
Some hold that merely removing the loose, outer leaves allows one to use the entire vegetable without further inspection, if the vegetable is U.S. grown. Nevertheless, it is still preferable to inspect three additional inner leaves and flush the remaining leaves in running water.[3] There is another view that holds that all leaves must be soaked in a vinegar solution and then individually inspected.[1]

METHOD D
Remove all soil by flushing in running water, since insects may appear as specks of dirt. A vegetable brush is helpful for cleaning. Inspect stalks

METHOD E
To clean florets, soak in lukewarm water (preferably a vinegar or salt water solution) in a lightly colored bowl. Run finger through the florets and agitate them in the water by holding on to the stem. Inspect the water. If insects are present, empty the water and repeat this procedure until the water is insect-free.[1,2] Rinse the vegetable before using.

Reprinted by permission of Rabbi Beryl Broyde

INDEX

225

226

In Memory of
Moshe and Chana Rubinstein z"l

who were an inspiration to their children
and their grandchildren all their lives

by their grandchildren
Rachel
Josh
David
Noah
Daniel
Talia
Aaron
Jeremy

❀ ❀ ❀

In Loving Memory of
Isadore "Ted" Levine

Of Blessed Memory

יצחק בן מאיר שמואל
תנצב"ה

by his children
Asher and Sharon Levine

and his grandchildren
Dovid Simcha
Esther Chaya
Meir Binyomin
Ruth Chana
Rivka Mariam

He was an inspiration to us all.

YASHER KOACH

to the following people who have helped
financially to produce this publication:

Mr. & Mrs. Roland Arnall

Mrs. Cheryl Barnert

Mr. Steve Berger

Rabbi & Mrs. Yankie Dinowitz

Mr. Mordechai Douglas

Rabbi & Mrs. Mendel Duchman

Mr. & Mrs. Bob Elman

Mr. & Mrs. George and Eliana Feigelstock

Mr. & Mrs. Jeff Feld

Mr. & Mrs. David Grashin

Dr. & Mrs. Ben Lesin

Rabbi & Mrs. George Lintz

Mr. & Mrs. Alex Pollak

Mr. & Mrs. Steve Ross

Mr. & Mrs. David Rubin

Mr. & Mrs. Irving Rubenstein

Mr. & Mrs. Ralph Rubenstein

Mr. & Mrs. Cary Samuels

Mr. & Mrs. Zev Stoll

Dr. & Mrs. Steve Suffin

YASHER KOACH
to the following people who have helped
financially to produce this publication:

Dr. & Mrs. Bruce Wasserman

Mr. & Mrs. Lyle Weisman

Dr. & Mrs. Ahuva Wernick

Mr. & Mrs. Barry Weiss

Mr. & Mrs. Mordechai Wolin

In honor of our grandchildren
by Sol and Ruthie Teichman

In honor of
Yolanda Arnall

In honor of
Alan Ives

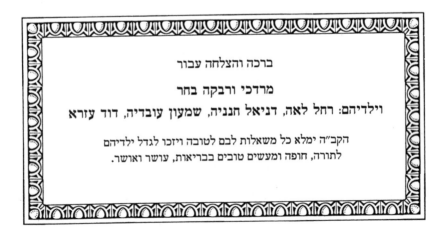

ברכה והצלחה עבור

מרדכי ורבקה בחר

וילדיהם: רחל לאה, דניאל חנניה, שמעון עובדיה, דוד עזרא

הקב״ה ימלא כל משאלות לבם לטובה ויזכו לגדל ילדיהם
לתורה, חופה ומעשים טובים בבריאות, עושר ואושר.

IN MEMORY OF

In loving memory of our dear mother
Aidel Eita Eisen z"l
Bas Reuven
תנצב"ה
by her children
Rabbi & Mrs. Eliezer Eidlitz
Mr. & Mrs. Sid Eidlitz
Mr. & Mrs. Sammy Weissman
❀ ❀ ❀
In loving memory of
Sam Teichman z"l
Lujza Teichman z"l
Isaac Noe z"l
by Sol & Ruthie Teichman
❀ ❀ ❀
In loving memory of
Chana Rubenstein z"l
who was an inspiration to her children and grandchildren in doing
Chesed and Maasim Tovim all her life
תנצב"ה
by Mr. & Mrs. Irving Rubenstein
Mr. Ralph Rubenstein
❀ ❀ ❀
In memory of
Naomi Barkoff Pesses z"l
by Dr. & Mrs. Martin Kay
❀ ❀ ❀
In memory of
Myer & Marcia Grashin
by their children and grandchildren
Mayer, Joshua, Ari, and Zach Grashin
David & Debbie Grashin

In memory of
Irving H. Ross
by Benjamin Wechselbaum
❊ ❊ ❊
In memory of
Isaac Mallel and Stella Jaffe
love, Ray, Ann, & David Mallel
❊ ❊ ❊
In memory of
Nora Isaac Ives and Clement Seroussi
love, Eddy & Dolly Ives and family
❊ ❊ ❊
In loving memory of
Rhona Duben
by the Wilshinsky family
❊ ❊ ❊
In loving memory of
Mike and Bernice Samuels
תׄנׄצׄבׄהׄ׳
by Cary and Joyce Samuels and family
❊ ❊ ❊
In memory of
Howard Steinmauer
צבי אלימלך בן אברהם לייב ז״ל
and Milton and Katie Donfeld
קרנדל בת דוב ז״ל
מיכאל בן אליעזר ז״ל
תׄנׄצׄבׄהׄ׳

In memory of
Eugene Arnall
יוסף יעקב בן ישעיה ז״ל